THE MAP BOOK

Outline Maps and Fact Sheets for States, Regions, and Countries

HARCOURT BRACE & COMPANY

Orlando Atlanta Austin Boston San Francisco Chicago Dallas

New York Toronto London

Visit The Learning Site at http://www.hbschool.com

To the Teacher

The Map Book is a tool to reinforce and extend the geographic knowledge of your students. It consists primarily of two elements: blank maps and fact sheets.

The Map Book can be used in a variety of ways at all grade levels. If your students are learning about locations of major political or geographic regions, have them color in these places on the appropriate blank map. For instance, students might color in your state on a map of the United States, and locate and label your state's capital.

As the students begin to study major cities, landforms, and rivers, they can use the fact sheets as a source of information about these features at the state, regional, national, or world level. Have the students use blank maps to write in capitals or major cities, or to draw and label physical features like mountains and rivers. Some students may want to make special maps showing major rivers of the world, major volcanoes, or the highest mountains.

As you study your own state or region, the students could use blank maps to make their own atlases. They might include one map showing cities, another showing mountains and rivers, and still another showing land use or resources.

The blank maps can be invaluable in helping students grasp historical changes. For instance, a sequence of maps could show territorial expansion or movements of people. Blank maps could be used to contrast political features of a region or country in different periods of time.

Another way to use *The Map Book* is to encourage students who are doing independent reports to include maps as part of their reports. A report on the Grand Canyon, for instance, could include the regional map of the Southwest with the location of the Grand Canyon identified. A student reporting on pyramids could identify the sites of the pyramids on a blank map of the Middle East: Southwest Asia and North Africa.

Printed in the United States of America

ISBN 0-15-310436-8

8 9 10 11 12 13 14 15   085   05 04 03 02

CONTENTS

MAPS AND FACTS

ALABAMA

0   20   40 Miles

0   25   50 Kilometers

FACTS ABOUT

ALABAMA

Population: 4,319,000

Capital: Montgomery

State flower: Camellia

State bird: Yellowhammer

State nickname: Heart of Dixie, Camellia State

Largest cities: Birmingham, Mobile, Montgomery, Huntsville, Tuscaloosa

Major land areas: Appalachian Mountains, Appalachian Plateau, Black Belt, Gulf Coastal Plain, Interior Low Plateau, Piedmont

Lowest point: Along the Gulf of Mexico, sea level

Highest point: Cheaha Mountain, 2,407 feet (734 m)

Major rivers: Alabama River, Black Warrior River, Cahaba River, Chattahoochee River, Coosa River, Mobile River, Tallapoosa River, Tennessee River, Tombigbee River

Major bodies of water: Gulf of Mexico, Guntersville Lake (artificial), Lewis Smith Lake (artificial), Martin Lake (artificial), Mississippi Sound, Mobile Bay, Perdido Bay, Walter F. George Lake (artificial), Weiss Lake (artificial), Wheeler Lake (artificial)

Climate: In January temperatures range from 40°F (4°C) to 60°F (16°C), and in July temperatures range from 73°F (23°C) to 91°F (33°C). The average yearly precipitation is 64 inches (163 cm).

Resources, industries, and products: Electronics, metals, paper, lumber, automotive tires, fishing, chickens, cattle, hogs, soybeans, cotton, peanuts

History: Spaniards explored Alabama in the sixteenth century. French Canadians set up the first permanent settlement in 1702. From 1763 to 1814, parts of the Alabama region were claimed by Britain, Spain, the United States, and the Creek Indians. In 1819 Alabama became the twenty-second state.

Historic sites and other attractions: The George Washington Carver Museum at Tuskegee University, the Alabama Space and Rocket Center, Russell Cave National Monument, Helen Keller's birthplace near Tuscumbia

Unusual facts: Russell Cave was inhabited as early as 6000 B.C. Montgomery was one capital of the Confederate States of America during the Civil War. The *Jupiter-C* rocket that carried the first United States satellite into space was developed in Huntsville.

Original American Indian groups: Alabama, Cherokee, Chickasaw, Choctaw, Creek, Hitchiti, Mobile, Muskogee

Harcourt Brace School Publishers

THE MAP BOOK

Name _____

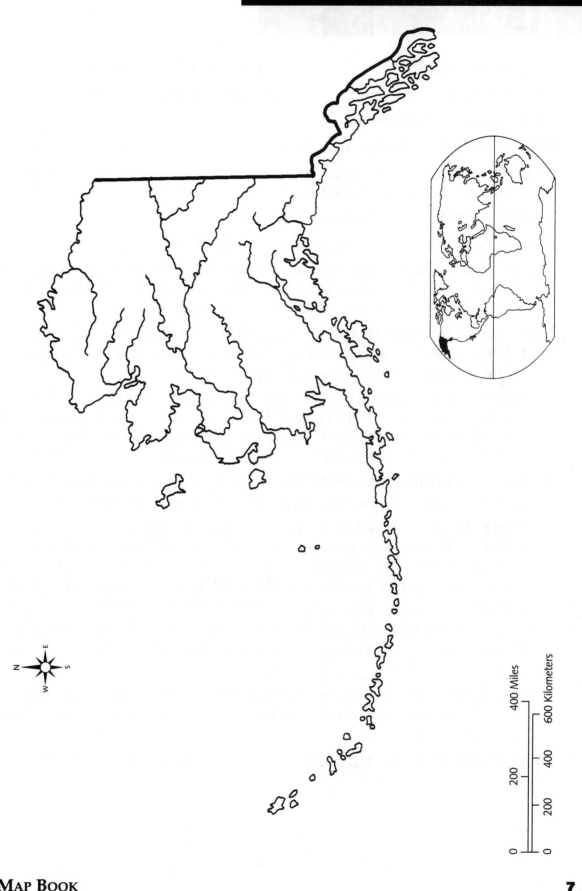

Harcourt Brace School Publishers

400 Miles

600 Kilometers

FACTS ABOUT
ALASKA

Population: 609,000

Capital: Juneau

State nickname: Last Frontier

State flower: Forget-me-not

State bird: Willow ptarmigan

Largest cities: Anchorage, Fairbanks, Juneau, College, Ninilchik, Sitka, Ketchikan

Major land areas: Alaska Range, Aleutian Islands, Alexander Archipelago, Arctic Plains, Brooks Range, Central Uplands and Lowlands, Seward Peninsula

Lowest point: Along the Pacific coast, sea level

Highest point: Mount McKinley, 20,320 feet (6,194 m)

Major rivers: Alsek River, Colville River, Copper River, Kobuk River, Koyukuk River, Kuskokwim River, Matanuska River, Noatak River, Stikine River, Susitna River, Taku River, Tanana River, Yukon River

Major bodies of water: Becharof Lake, Bering Strait, Bristol Bay, Chukchi Sea, Cook Inlet, Gulf of Alaska, Iliamna Lake, Kotzebue Sound, Kuskokwim Bay, Norton Sound, Selawik Lake, Teshekpuk Lake

Climate: In the south temperatures range from 8°F (-13°C) to 21°F (-6°C) in January and from 52°F (11°C) to 65°F (18°C) in July. In the north temperatures range from -19°F (-28°C) to -7°F (-22°C) in January and from 34°F (1°C) to 45°F (7°C) in July. The average yearly precipitation is 16 inches (41 cm).

Resources, industries, and products: Oil, food processing, lumber products, barley, hay, natural gas, tourism, mining, potatoes, furs, gold, fishing

History: Vitus Bering, a Danish explorer working for Russia, was the first European in Alaska, in 1741. Russia established settlements and governed the region until 1867, when the United States bought it for $7.2 million. After the discovery of gold in 1896, a gold rush began. Declared a United States territory in 1912, Alaska became the forty-ninth state in 1959.

Historic sites and other attractions: Portage Glacier, Denali National Park, Glacier Bay National Park, Sitka National Historical Park, Pribilof Island fur seal rookeries, Ketchikan totem poles

Unusual facts: Alaska is the largest state and has the tallest mountain in North America, Mount McKinley. Alaska has the largest salmon-canning industry in the United States.

Original Native American groups: Aleut, Athabaskan, Haida, Inuit, Tlingit

Harcourt Brace School Publishers

THE MAP BOOK

Name _____

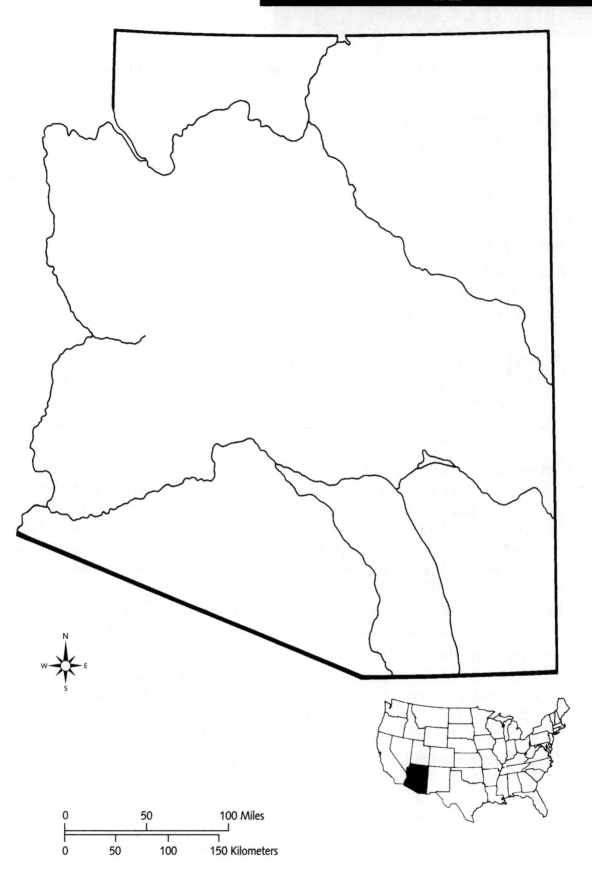

0   50   100 Miles

0   50   100   150 Kilometers

Harcourt Brace School Publishers

THE MAP BOOK

Name _____

Population: 4,554,000

State flower: Saguaro (Giant cactus)

Capital: Phoenix

State bird: Cactus wren

State nickname: Grand Canyon State

Largest cities: Phoenix, Tucson, Mesa, Glendale, Tempe, Scottsdale

Major land areas: Basin and Range Region, Colorado Plateau, Grand Canyon, Painted Desert, Sonoran Desert

Lowest point: In Yuma County, 70 feet (21 m) above sea level

Highest point: Humphreys Peak, 12,633 feet (3,851 m)

Major rivers: Bill Williams River, Colorado River, Gila River, Little Colorado River, San Pedro River, Santa Cruz River

Major bodies of water: Lake Havasu, Lake Mead, Lake Mojave, Lake Powell, San Carlos Lake, Theodore Roosevelt Lake (all artificial)

Climate: In January temperatures range from 41°F (5°C) to 66°F (19°C), and in July temperatures range from 81°F (27°C) to 106°F (41°C). The average yearly precipitation is 8 inches (20 cm).

Resources, industries, and products: Manufacturing, tourism, electronics, cattle, copper, cotton, mining

History: In the sixteenth century, Spanish explorers searched Arizona for treasure. In the seventeenth century, Roman Catholic missions were established. Spain gave the territory to Mexico in 1821. Following the Mexican War in 1848, Mexico gave the United States an area that included most of present-day Arizona. In 1853 the Gadsden Purchase added more territory to Arizona. In 1886 Geronimo surrendered, ending the Apache wars. In 1912 Arizona became the forty-eighth state.

Historic sites and other attractions: Grand Canyon, Painted Desert, Petrified Forest, Meteor Crater, San Xavier del Bac Mission, London Bridge

Unusual facts: Between 1950 and 1970, Arizona's population almost quadrupled because of the development of air conditioning. The Grand Canyon is one of the Seven Wonders of the World. Oraibi, built by Hopi Indians in the twelfth century, is the oldest continuously inhabited settlement in the United States. Arizona has more national monuments than any other state.

Original American Indian groups: Apache, Havasupai, Hopi, Mojave, Navajo, Papago, Pima, Yarapai, Yuma

Harcourt Brace School Publishers

Name _____

ARKANSAS

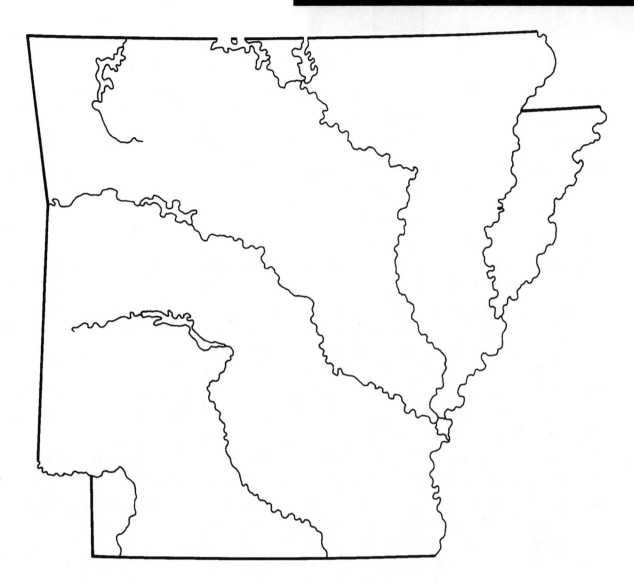

Harcourt Brace School Publishers

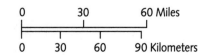

| 0 | 30 | 60 Miles |
| 0 | 30 | 60 | 90 Kilometers |

FACTS ABOUT
ARKANSAS

Population: 2,522,000

Capital: Little Rock

State nickname: Land of Opportunity

State flower: Apple blossom

State bird: Mockingbird

Largest cities: Little Rock, Fort Smith, North Little Rock, Pine Bluff, Fayetteville

Major land areas: Arkansas Valley, Gulf Coastal Plain, Mississippi Alluvial Plain, Ouachita Mountains, Ozark Plateau

Lowest point: Ouachita River, 55 Feet (17 m) above sea level

Highest point: Magazine Mountain, 2,753 feet (839 m)

Major rivers: Arkansas River, Mississippi River, Ouachita River, Red River, St. Francis River, White River

Major bodies of water: Beaver Lake, Bull Shoals Lake, Lake Catherine (artificial), Lake Dardanelle (artificial), Greers Ferry Lake, Lake Hamilton (artificial), Lake Ouachita (artificial), McClellan-Kerr Arkansas River Navigation System (artificial), Millwood Lake, Norfork Lake (artificial)

Climate: In January temperatures range from 29°F (-2°C) to 49°F (9°C), and in July temperatures range from 72°F (22°C) to 92°F (33°C). The average yearly precipitation is 49 inches (124 cm).

Resources, industries, and products: Manufacturing, agriculture, tourism, lumber, food processing, chemicals, cattle, soybeans, rice, cotton

History: In 1541 Hernando de Soto of Spain explored the territory. In 1673 Jolliet and Marquette of France traveled down the Mississippi River as far south as the mouth of the Arkansas River. In 1682 France claimed the region. The United States gained Arkansas in the Louisiana Purchase, in 1803. In 1836 Arkansas became the twenty-fifth state.

Historic sites and other attractions: Hot Springs National Park, Blanchard Springs Caverns, Crater of Diamonds, Mammoth Spring, Pea Ridge National Military Park

Unusual facts: Arkansas has the only major diamond field in the United States. The oldest newspaper west of the Mississippi River is the Arkansas *Gazette*, founded in 1819.

Original American Indian groups: Caddo, Cahinnio, Choctaw, Kaskinampo, Osage, Quapaw

Harcourt Brace School Publishers

CALIFORNIA

N
W ☼ E
S

0   50   100 Miles

0   50   100   150 Kilometers

Harcourt Brace School Publishers

Name _____

CALIFORNIA

Population: 32,268,000

Capital: Sacramento

State nickname: Golden State

State flower: Golden poppy

State bird: California valley quail

Largest cities: Los Angeles, San Diego, San Jose, San Francisco, Long Beach

Major land areas: Basin and Range Region, Cascade Range, Central Valley, Coast Ranges, Imperial Valley, Sierra Nevada

Lowest point: Death Valley, 282 feet (86 m) below sea level

Highest point: Mount Whitney, 14,495 feet (4,418 m)

Major rivers: Colorado River, Feather River, Mokelumne River, Pit River, Sacramento River, San Joaquin River

Major bodies of water: Gulf of Santa Catalina, Lake Tahoe, Monterey Bay, Salton Sea, San Diego Bay, San Francisco Bay, Shasta Lake

Climate: In January temperatures in Los Angeles range from 49°F (9°C) to 68°F (20°C) and in July from 65°F (18°C) to 84°F (29°C). In January temperatures in San Francisco range from 42°F (6°C) to 56°F (13°C) and in July from 54°F (12°C) to 72°F (22°C). In Los Angeles the average yearly precipitation is 15 inches (38 cm) and in San Francisco the average is 20 inches (51 cm).

Resources, industries, and products: Agriculture, electronics, trade, boron, cattle, chickens, grapes, oranges, flowers, tomatoes, nuts, fishing, tourism

History: Spain sent explorers to California in the sixteenth century. In the eighteenth century, Spaniards settled in present-day San Francisco. In 1822 California became a Mexican province. Mexico lost California to the United States after the Mexican War in 1848. That year, the discovery of gold led to the 1849 gold rush. In 1850 California became the thirty-first state.

Historic sites and other attractions: Redwood National Park, Sequoia National Park, San Diego Zoo, Muir Woods, Mojave Desert, La Brea Tar Pits, Yosemite National Park

Unusual facts: The highest temperature ever recorded in the United States was 134°F (57°C), in Death Valley in 1913. Ribbon Falls in Yosemite National Park is the highest waterfall in North America. The Howard Libby redwood tree is the tallest living plant in the world.

Original American Indian groups: Achomawi, Chumash, Cochimi, Costano, Diequeno, Gabrielmo, Kamia, Luiseno, Maidu, Miwok, Pomo, Serrano, Shasta, Wailaki, Wappo, Wintun, Yana, Yokuts, Yuki

Harcourt Brace School Publishers

Name _____

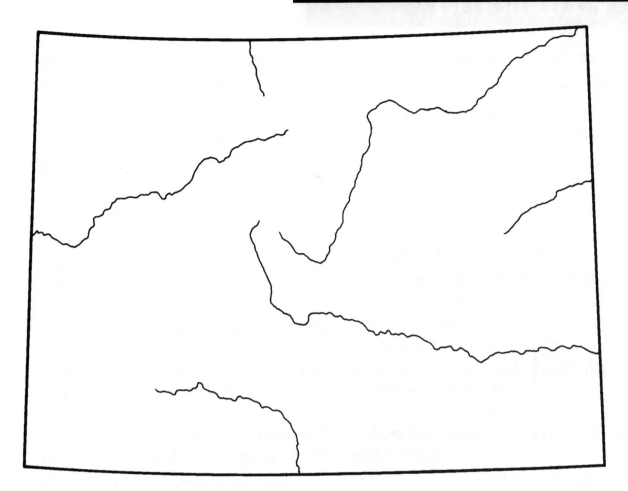

Harcourt Brace School Publishers

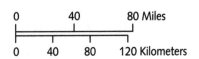

FACTS ABOUT

COLORADO

Population: 3,892,000

Capital: Denver

State nickname: Centennial State

State flower: Rocky Mountain columbine

State bird: Lark bunting

Largest cities: Denver, Colorado Springs, Aurora, Lakewood, Pueblo

Major land areas: Colorado Plateau, Great Plains, Rocky Mountains, Wyoming Basin

Lowest point: Along the Arkansas River in Prowers County, 3,350 feet (1,021 m) above sea level

Highest point: Mount Elbert, 14,433 feet (4,399 m)

Major rivers: Arkansas River, Colorado River, North Platte River, Republican River, Rio Grande, South Platte River

Major bodies of water: Blue Mesa Reservoir, Grand Lake, John Martin Reservoir, Lake Granby, Meredith Lake, Nee Reservoirs

Climate: In January temperatures range from 16°F (-9° C) to 43° F (6°C), and in July temperatures range from 59°F (15°C) to 88°F (31°C). The average yearly precipitation is 15 inches (38 cm).

Resources, industries, and products: Agriculture, government, aerospace, electronics, timber, cattle, wheat, corn, sugar beets, peaches, pears, tourism

History: Spaniards searched Colorado for gold in the sixteenth century. In 1682 France claimed eastern Colorado. In 1803 the United States bought the eastern and central regions of Colorado in the Louisiana Purchase. The United States gained the western portion in the Mexican War (1846–1848). In 1858 gold was discovered near present-day Denver. In 1876 Colorado became the thirty-eighth state.

Historic sites and other attractions: Pikes Peak, Rocky Mountain National Park, Mesa Verde National Park, Garden of the Gods, Dinosaur National Monument

Unusual facts: More than one-third of Colorado's land is owned by the federal government. The highest road in the United States climbs to Mount Evans. The world's highest suspension bridge crosses Royal Gorge. Leadville is the highest city in the United States.

Original American Indian groups: Arapaho, Cheyenne, Jicarilla, Navajo, Ute

CONNECTICUT

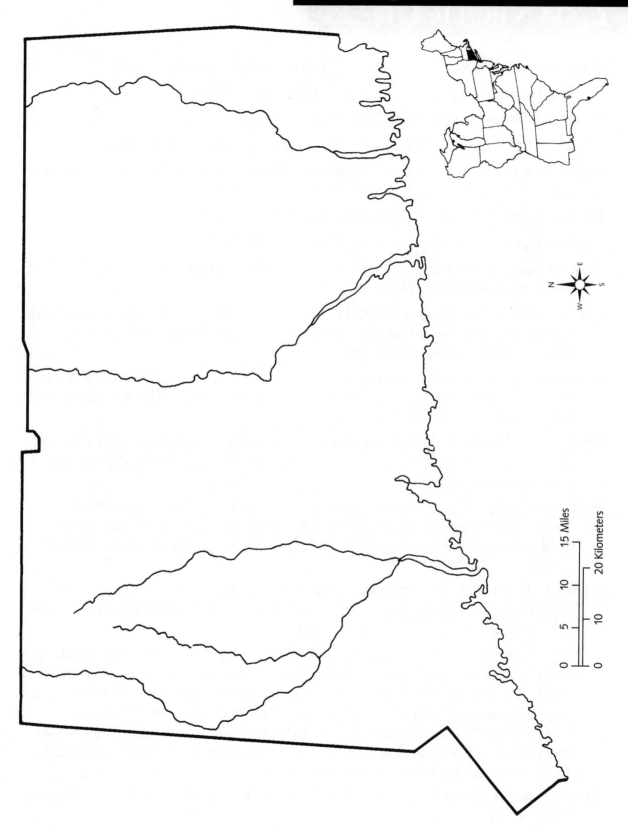

15 Miles

20 Kilometers

Harcourt Brace School Publishers

FACTS ABOUT
CONNECTICUT

Population: 3,269,000

Capital: Hartford

State flower: Mountain laurel

State bird: Robin

State nicknames: Constitution State, Nutmeg State

Largest cities: Bridgeport, Hartford, New Haven, Waterbury, Stamford

Major land areas: Appalachian Mountains, Atlantic Coastal Plain, Connecticut Valley Lowland, New England Upland

Lowest point: Along the Long Island Sound shore, sea level

Highest point: South slope of Mount Frissel, 2,380 feet (725 m)

Major rivers: Connecticut River, Housatonic River, Naugatuck River, Quinebaug River, Shepaug River, Thames River

Major bodies of water: Bantam Lake, Barkhamsted Reservoir, Candlewood Lake (artificial), Long Island Sound, Mansfield Hollow Lake, Pachaug Pond, Shenipsit Lake, Waramaug Lake

Climate: In January temperatures range from 16°F (-9°C) to 33°F (1°C), and in July temperatures range from 62°F (17°C) to 85°F (29°C). The average yearly precipitation is 44 inches (112 cm).

Resources, industries, and products: Manufacturing, insurance, helicopters, jet engines, submarines, mushrooms, sweet corn, fishing, electrical products, sand, gravel, apples

History: In 1614 a Dutch explorer claimed the region. By 1634 people from Plymouth Bay had started English settlements along the Connecticut River. In 1674 the English drove out the Dutch. In 1788 Connecticut became the fifth state.

Historic sites and other attractions: Mark Twain House, Peabody Museum, Mystic Seaport, Mystic Marine Life Aquarium, Yale University's Art Gallery, P. T. Barnum Museum, Groton Monument

Unusual facts: America's first law school was founded in Litchfield in 1784. The *Nautilus*, the first nuclear submarine, was built in 1954 at Groton. In the early 1800s, Eli Whitney pioneered the use of interchangeable parts in manufacturing in Hamden. The first American school for the deaf was founded in Hartford in 1817 by Thomas H. Gallaudet. Connecticut is sometimes called the Provision State because it provided so many supplies to Washington's troops during the American Revolution.

Original American Indian groups: Mahican, Mohegan, Niantic, Nitmuc, Pequot, Wappinger

Harcourt Brace School Publishers

Name _____

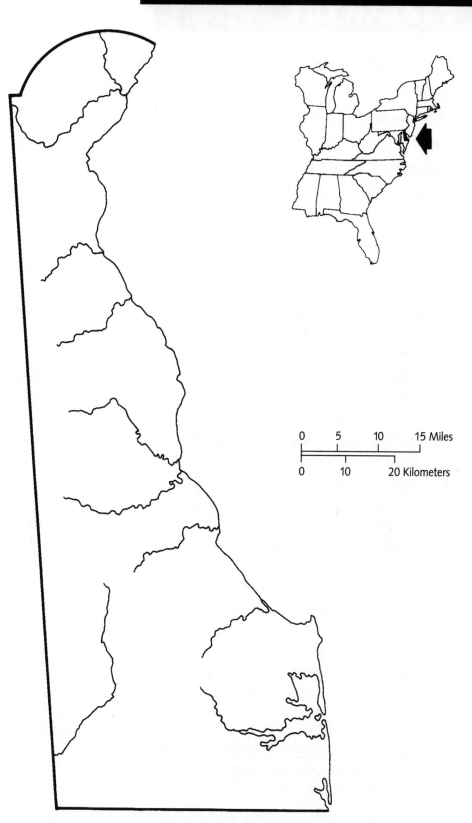

0   5   10   15 Miles

0   10   20 Kilometers

Harcourt Brace School Publishers

FACTS ABOUT
DELAWARE

Population: 731,000

Capital: Dover

State nicknames: First State, Diamond State

Largest cities: Wilmington, Dover, Newark, Milford, Seaford

Major land areas: Atlantic Coastal Plain, Piedmont

Lowest point: Along the Atlantic coast, sea level

Highest point: Ebright Road in New Castle County, 442 feet (135 m)

Major rivers: Appoquinimink Creek, Brandywine Creek, Broadkill River, Christina River, Delaware River, Indian River, Mispillion River, Murderkill River, Nanticoke River, St. Jones River, Smyrna River

Major bodies of water: Chesapeake and Delaware Canal, Delaware Bay, Indian River Bay, Rehoboth Bay

Climate: In January temperatures range from 22°F (-6°C) to 39°F (4°C), and in July temperatures range from 67°F (19°C) to 86°F (30°C). The coastal areas are an average of 10°F (6°C) cooler than the inland regions. The average yearly precipitation is 41 inches (104 cm).

Resources, industries, and products: Chemicals, agriculture, shellfish, poultry, auto assembly, nylon, luggage, watermelons, tourism, fishing, soybeans, corn

History: In 1609 Henry Hudson explored Delaware for the Dutch. In 1638 Swedish settlers came to the Delaware region. They established New Sweden, the region's first permanent European settlement. Later, settlers from Finland helped expand the colony northward. In 1682 the English made the Delaware region part of the Pennsylvania Colony. Delaware split away in 1704. In 1787 Delaware became the first state.

Historic sites and other attractions: Ft. Christina Monument, Henry Francis du Pont Winterthur Museum, Old Dutch House, Rehoboth Beach, Hagley Museum Historic Site

Unusual facts: Nylon, first introduced to the public in 1938, was invented in the Du Pont Laboratories in Delaware. Delaware is the second-smallest state. Delaware is the only state whose counties are divided into areas called "hundreds." Members of New Sweden, the first permanent colony in Delaware, founded in 1638, built the first log cabins in America. Because several large chemical companies are located in or near Wilmington, this city is sometimes called the Chemical Capital of the World.

Original American Indian groups: Delaware, Nanticoke

State flower: Peach blossom

State bird: Blue hen chicken

Harcourt Brace School Publishers

Name _____

N
W · E
S

Harcourt Brace School Publishers

0   50   100 Miles
0   50   100   150 Kilometers

Name _____

F LORIDA

Population: 14,653,000

Capital: Tallahassee

State nickname: Sunshine State

State flower: Orange blossom

State bird: Mockingbird

Largest cities: Jacksonville, Miami, Tampa, St. Petersburg, Hialeah

Major land areas: Atlantic Coastal Plain, Everglades, Florida Uplands, Gulf Coastal Plain

Lowest point: Along the Atlantic Ocean, sea level

Highest point: In Walton County, 345 feet (105 m)

Major rivers: Apalachicola River, Caloosahatchee River, Chattahoochee River, Kissimmee River, Peace River, Perdido River, St. Johns River, St. Marys River, Suwannee River

Major bodies of water: Apalachee Bay, Charlotte Harbor, Florida Bay, Gulf of Mexico, Lake George, Lake Kissimmee, Lake Okeechobee, Pensacola Bay, Tampa Bay

Climate: In January temperatures in Miami, in the south of Florida, range from 59°F (15°C) to 75°F (24°C) and in Jacksonville, in the north, temperatures range from 41°F (5°C) to 64°F (18°C). In July temperatures in Miami range from 76°F (24°C) to 89°F (32°C) and in Jacksonville temperatures range from 72°F (22°C) to 91°F (33°C). Yearly precipitation in Miami averages 56 inches (142 cm) and in Jacksonville averages 51 inches (130 cm).

Resources, industries, and products: Tourism, international trade, electronics, printing and publishing, citrus fruits, sugarcane, cattle, fishing, strawberries, melons

History: In 1513 Ponce de León explored Florida, looking for a legendary fountain of youth. He claimed the region for Spain. In 1763 Spain gave the region to England in exchange for Cuba. In 1783 Spain recaptured Florida. Spain gave the territory to the United States in 1819. Florida became the twenty-seventh state in 1845.

Historic sites and other attractions: Kennedy Space Center, Everglades National Park, John Pennekamp Coral Reef State Park, Castillo de San Marcos National Monument

Unusual facts: St. Augustine, founded in 1565, is the oldest city in the United States. Florida has the longest coastline of any state except Alaska. The nation's first satellite, *Explorer I*, was launched from Cape Canaveral in 1958. St. Petersburg once had 768 sunny days in a row.

Original American Indian groups: Apalachee, Calusa, Pensacola, Seminole, Timucuan, Tunica

Harcourt Brace School Publishers

THE MAP BOOK

Name _____

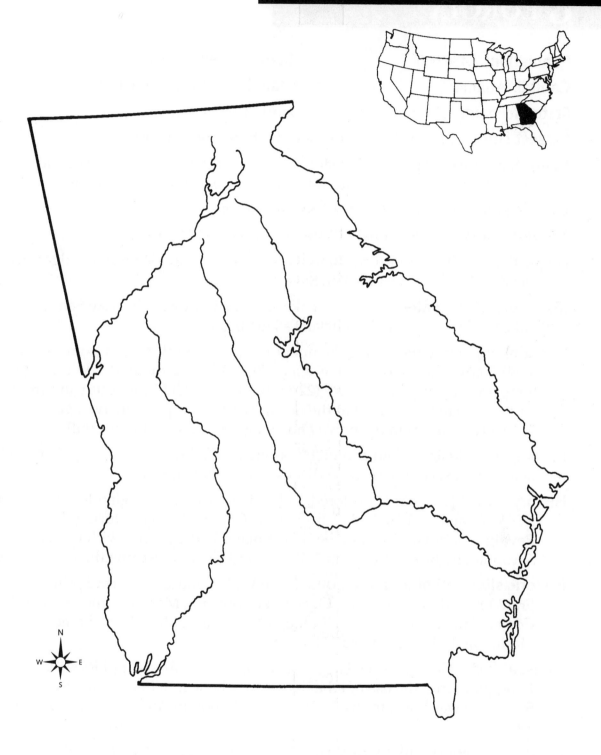

N
W ✦ E
S

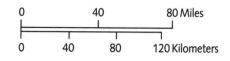

Harcourt Brace School Publishers

Name _____

FACTS ABOUT

GEORGIA

Population: 7,486,000

Capital: Atlanta

State flower: Cherokee rose

State bird: Brown thrasher

State nicknames: Empire State of the South, Peach State

Largest cities: Atlanta, Columbus, Savannah, Macon, Albany

Major land areas: Appalachian Mountains, Appalachian Plateau, Atlantic Coastal Plain, Blue Ridge Mountains, Gulf Coastal Plain, Piedmont

Lowest point: Along the Atlantic coast, sea level

Highest point: Brasstown Bald Mountain, 4,784 feet (1,458 m)

Major rivers: Altamaha River, Chattahoochee River, Flint River, Ocmulgee River, Oconee River, St. Marys River, Savannah River

Major bodies of water: Allatoona Lake, Clark Hill Reservoir, Lake Seminole, Lake Sidney Lanier, Lake Sinclair (all artificial)

Climate: In January the average temperature in the south ranges from 38°F (3°C) to 60°F (16°C) and from 32°F (0°C) to 50°F (10°C) in the north. In July the temperature ranges from 72°F (22°C) to 91°F (33°C) in the south and from 70°F (21°C) to 88°F (31°C) in the north. Yearly precipitation averages 51 inches (130 cm) in the north and 49 inches (124 cm) in the south.

Resources, industries, and products: Services, retail trade, textiles, paper products, peanuts, cotton, corn, soybeans, cattle, timber, peaches

History: In 1540 Spaniards explored and claimed Georgia. England then claimed it in 1629 and by 1732 had chartered the Georgia Colony. During the Revolutionary War, Georgia became a major battleground with the capture of Savannah by British troops in 1778. In 1788 Georgia became the fourth state.

Historic sites and other attractions: Little White House in Warm Springs (where Franklin D. Roosevelt died), Okefenokee Swamp, Martin Luther King, Jr. Center, Yamacraw Bluff, Chattanooga National Military Park, Stone Mountain, Dahlonega Gold Museum

Unusual facts: Georgia is the largest state east of the Mississippi River. Crawford Long pioneered the use of ether as an anesthetic in Jefferson, in 1842. Savannah was home to the first Girl Scout troop in America, organized in 1912.

Original American Indian groups: Apalachicola, Chiaha, Creek, Guale, Hitchiti, Oconee, Tamathli, Yamasee, Yuchi

Harcourt Brace School Publishers

Name _____

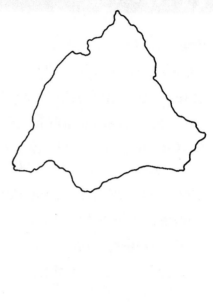

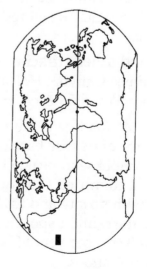

80 Miles

120 Kilometers

40

80

40

0

0

Harcourt Brace School Publishers

FACTS ABOUT
*H*AWAII

Population: 1,186,000

Capital: Honolulu

State nickname: Aloha State

Largest cities: Honolulu, Hilo, Kailua, Kaneohe, Waipahu

Major land areas: Hawaii, Kahoolawe, Kauai, Lanai, Maui, Molokai, Niihau, Oahu (all islands of Hawaii)

Lowest point: Along the Pacific Ocean, sea level

Highest point: Mauna Kea on Hawaii, 13,796 feet (4,205 m)

Major rivers: None

Major bodies of water: Hilo Bay, Kaneohe Bay, Kauai Channel, Mamala Bay, Pearl Harbor

State flower: Yellow hibiscus

State bird: Hawaiian goose

Climate: In January temperatures in Hawaii's lowlands range from 66°F (19°C) to 80°F (27°C). In July temperatures range from 74°F (23°C) to 88°F (31°C). Precipitation varies from 300 inches (762 cm) a year in the mountains to less than 22 inches (56 cm) in the lowlands.

Resources, industries, and products: Tourism, government, sugar, pineapples, fishing, motion pictures, stone, cattle, coffee, clothing, printing and publishing

History: Captain James Cook reached Hawaii in 1778. In 1795 King Kamehameha I united and ruled most of the islands. During the nineteenth century, sugar and pineapple plantations grew rapidly. In 1893 the Hawaiian monarchy was toppled, and Hawaii became an independent republic one year later. In 1898 the United States annexed the islands. When Japan attacked Pearl Harbor in 1941, the United States entered World War II. In 1959 Hawaii became the fiftieth state.

Historic sites and other attractions: James Cook Monument, Polynesian Cultural Center, Waimea Canyon, Haleakala National Park, U.S.S. *Arizona* Memorial at Pearl Harbor, Waikiki Beach, Hawaii Volcanoes National Park, Diamond Head

Unusual facts: Mauna Kea is the world's highest island peak when measured from the edge of its true base on the ocean floor, at a height of 32,000 feet (9,754 m) from base to peak. Hawaii is one of three states that have been independent countries. (The other two are Texas and Vermont.) Hawaii is the only state with no city and town governments. Mount Waialeale on the island of Kauai is the rainiest spot in the world. (It rains there an average of 460 inches [1,168 cm] per year.) Hawaii is the only state in the nation totally formed by volcanoes.

Original Native American group: Polynesian

Harcourt Brace School Publishers

THE MAP BOOK

Name _____

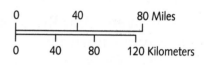

0   40   80 Miles

0   40   80   120 Kilometers

Harcourt Brace School Publishers

Name _____

*I*DAHO

Population: 1,210,000

Capital: Boise

State nickname: Gem State

State flower: Syringa (mock orange)

State bird: Mountain bluebird

Largest cities: Boise, Pocatello, Idaho Falls, Nampa, Lewiston, Twin Falls

Major land areas: Basin and Range Region, Columbia Plateau, Rocky Mountains

Lowest point: Snake River at Lewiston, 710 feet (216 m) above sea level

Highest point: Borah Peak, 12,662 feet (3,859 m)

Major rivers: Bear River, Big Wood River, Blackfoot River, Boise River, Bruneau River, Clearwater River, Coeur d'Alene River, Kootenai River, Payette River, Pend Oreille River, Salmon River, Snake River, Spokane River, Weiser River

Major bodies of water: American Falls Reservoir, Bear Lake, Coeur d'Alene Lake, Crystal Lake Falls, Pend Oreille Lake, Priest Lake, Shoshone Falls

Climate: In January temperatures range from 22°F (-6°C) to 36°F (2°C), and in July temperatures range from 58°F (14°C) to 90°F (32°C). The average yearly precipitation is 12 inches (30 cm) throughout the state.

Resources, industries, and products: Agriculture, processed foods, tourism, lumber, potatoes, sugar beets, barley, cattle, mining, silver, lead

History: In 1805 Lewis and Clark passed through Idaho on their way to the Pacific Coast. In 1809 a fur-trading post was established. By 1860 Idaho had its first American settlement. The discovery of gold there in 1862 brought many new settlers. In 1863 Congress established the Idaho Territory. In 1890 Idaho became the forty-third state.

Historic sites and other attractions: Hells Canyon, Craters of the Moon National Monument, Old Fort Hall, Crystal Falls Cave, Sun Valley, Shoshone Falls, World Center for Birds of Prey

Unusual facts: Idaho has the largest silver mine in the United States. Hells Canyon is the deepest canyon in the United States, with an average depth of 1 mile (1.6 km). Idaho ranks first among the states in potato production. The town of Arco was the first town in the country to be lit by electricity from a nuclear power source.

Original American Indian groups: Bannock, Kalispel, Nez Perce, Northern Shoshoni, Skitswish, Western Shoshoni

THE MAP BOOK

Name _____

Harcourt Brace School Publishers

```
0          30          60 Miles
|----|----|----|----|----|

0     30     60     90 Kilometers
|----|----|----|----|----|----|
```

THE MAP BOOK

FACTS ABOUT
*I*LLINOIS

Population: 11,895,000

Capital: Springfield

State flower: Native violet

State bird: Cardinal

State nicknames: Prairie State, Land of Lincoln

Largest cities: Chicago, Rockford, Peoria, Springfield, Aurora, Decatur

Major land areas: Central Plains, Interior Low Plateau, Shawnee Hills

Lowest point: Along the Mississippi River in Alexander County, 279 feet (85 m) above sea level

Highest point: Charles Mound, 1,235 feet (376 m)

Major rivers: Chicago River, Des Plaines River, Fox River, Illinois River, Kaskaskia River, Mississippi River, Ohio River, Rock River, Sangamon River, Spoon River, Wabash River

Major bodies of water: Carlyle Lake (artificial), Crab Orchard Lake (artificial), Lake Michigan, Lake Shelbyville, Rend Lake, Senachwine Lake, Springfield Lake (artificial)

Climate: In the north temperatures range from 13°F (-11°C) to 29°F (-2°C) in January and from 63°F (17°C) to 84°F (29°C) in July. Southern Illinois temperatures range from 11°F (-12°C) to 28°F (-2°C) in January and from 65°F (18°C) to 86°F (30°C) in July. The average yearly precipitation is 39 inches (99 cm) in the south and 36 inches (91 cm) in the north.

Resources, industries, and products: Manufacturing, travel, agriculture, machinery, health care, insurance, electronic equipment, cattle, hogs, corn, soybeans

History: Illinois was explored by the French in 1673 and became part of the French colony of Louisiana in 1717. Britain won the territory from France in 1763. It became Virginia Territory in 1778, a part of the Northwest Territory in 1787, and Indiana Territory in 1800. In 1818 Illinois became the twenty-first state.

Historic sites and other attractions: Abraham Lincoln's home in Springfield, Black Hawk Statue in Lowden National Park, Ulysses S. Grant's home, Vandalia Court House, Dickson Mounds Museum, Crab Orchard Wildlife Refuge

Unusual facts: Prehistoric Indian "Mound Builders" constructed more than 10,000 mounds in Illinois, the largest prehistoric earthworks in the United States. Enrico Fermi and other scientists at the University of Chicago set off the first sustained nuclear reaction in 1942. Chicago has the largest post office in the United States.

Original American Indian groups: Illinois, Kickapoo, Miami, Sauk

Harcourt Brace School Publishers

THE MAP BOOK

Name _____

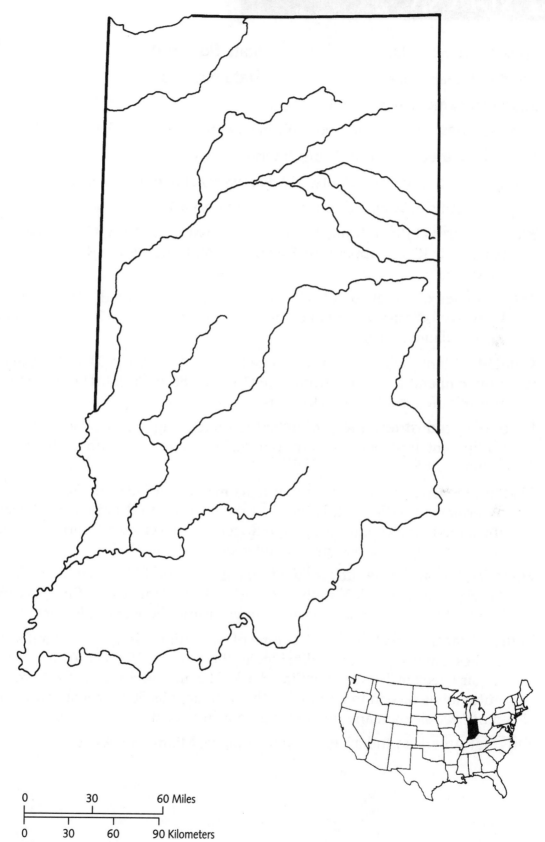

N
W   E
S

Harcourt Brace School Publishers

0   30   60 Miles

0   30   60   90 Kilometers

THE MAP BOOK

FACTS ABOUT

*I*NDIANA

Population: 5,864,000

Capital: Indianapolis

State nickname: Hoosier State

State flower: Peony

State bird: Cardinal

Largest cities: Indianapolis, Fort Wayne, Evansville, Gary, South Bend

Major land areas: Central Plains, Interior Low Plateau

Lowest point: In Posey County, 320 feet (98 m) above sea level

Highest point: In Wayne County, 1,257 feet (383 m)

Major rivers: Eel River, Kankakee River, Mississinewa River, Ohio River, Salamonie River, Tippecanoe River, Wabash River, White River, Whitewater River

Major bodies of water: Brookville Lake, Geist Reservoir, Lake Michigan, Lake Wawasee, Mississinewa Lake, Monroe Reservoir, Morse Reservoir, Patoka Lake, Salamonie Lake

Climate: In January temperatures range from 17°F (-8°C) to 34°F (1°C), and in July temperatures range from 65°F (18°C) to 86°F (30°C). The average yearly precipitation is 40 inches (102 cm).

Resources, industries, and products: Manufacturing, electrical and electronic equipment, transportation equipment, hogs, corn, soybeans, wheat, hay, fishing, cattle

History: French explorers reached Indiana in 1679. In 1731 the French established a permanent settlement. France lost the territory to Britain in 1763. During the American Revolution, George Rogers Clark seized the territory from the British. Indiana became the nineteenth state in 1816.

Historic sites and other attractions: Lincoln Boyhood National Memorial, George Rogers Clark National Historical Park, Tippecanoe Sites, Wyandotte Cave, Hoosier National Forest, Conner Prairie Pioneer Settlement

Unusual facts: Gary, Indiana, has some of the nation's largest steel mills. The longest single-span covered bridge in the country, 207 feet (63 m), crosses Sugar Creek in Turkey Run State Park. The annual 500-mile (800-km) automobile race in Indianapolis (the Indianapolis 500) probably attracts more people than any other single sporting event in the nation.

Original American Indian groups: Chippewa, Miami, Shawnee

Harcourt Brace School Publishers

THE MAP BOOK

Name _____

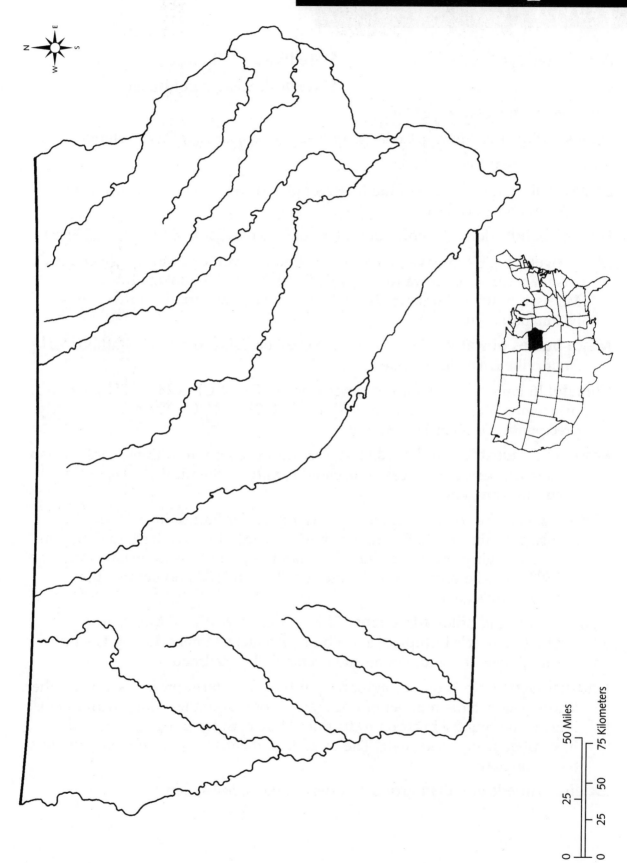

N E
W S

Harcourt Brace School Publishers

50 Miles
75 Kilometers
25
50
0 25 25
0

FACTS ABOUT
*I*OWA

Population: 2,852,000

Capital: Des Moines

State nickname: Hawkeye State

State flower: Wild rose

State bird: Eastern goldfinch

Largest cities: Des Moines, Cedar Rapids, Davenport, Sioux City, Waterloo

Major land area: Central Plains

Lowest point: The junction of the Mississippi and Des Moines rivers, 480 feet (146 m) above sea level

Highest point: Along the north boundary of Osceola County, 1,670 feet (509 m)

Major rivers: Big Sioux River, Boyer River, Cedar River, Des Moines River, East Nishnabotna River, Iowa River, Little Sioux River, Maquoketa River, Mississippi River, Missouri River, Turkey River, Wapsipinicon River, West Nishnabotna River

Major bodies of water: Clear Lake, Lake Okoboji, Lake Red Rock, Rathbun Lake, Saylorville Lake, Spirit Lake

Climate: In January temperatures range from 11°F (-12°C) to 28°F (-2°C) and in July temperatures range from 67°F (19°C) to 87°F (31°C). The average yearly precipitation is 33 inches (84 cm).

Resources, industries, and products: Agriculture, communications, construction, farm machinery, appliances, household furniture, chemicals, hogs, cattle, soybeans, corn, oats

History: French explorers claimed the Iowa region for France in 1673. In 1762 France gave the area to Spain, which in turn gave the area back to France in 1800. The United States purchased the land as part of the Louisiana Purchase in 1803. Iowa became a United States territory in 1838 and became the twenty-ninth state in 1846.

Historic sites and other attractions: Effigy Mounds National Monument, Herbert Hoover's birthplace and library, Amana Colonies, Living History Farms, Adventureland, Boone and Scenic Valley Railroad

Unusual facts: Iowa is the second-largest producer of farm products. Iowa is the leading state in the number of hogs raised for marketing. Along with Illinois, it leads the country in corn production. More corn for popping is raised in Iowa than in any other state. The word *Iowa* means "beautiful word" in the Sioux language.

Original American Indian groups: Eastern Dakota, Iowa, Sautee

Harcourt Brace School Publishers

THE MAP BOOK

Name _____

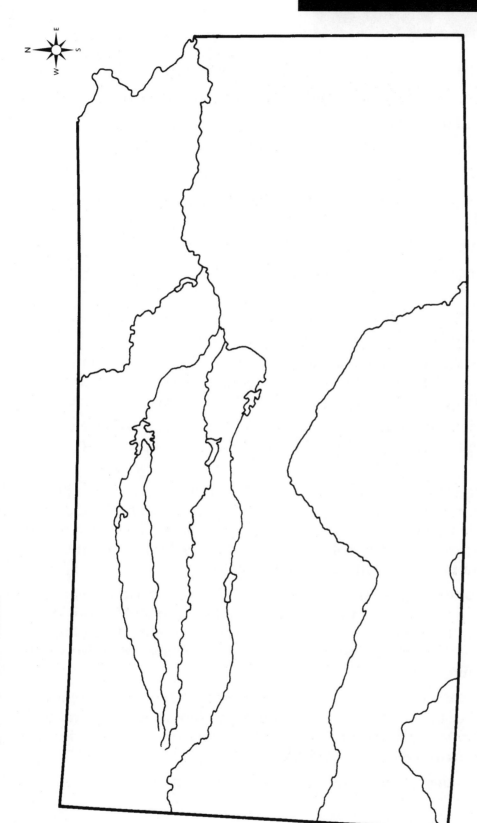

THE MAP BOOK

FACTS ABOUT
KANSAS

Population: 2,594,000

Capital: Topeka

State nickname: Sunflower State

State flower: Native sunflower

State bird: Western meadowlark

Largest cities: Wichita, Kansas City, Topeka, Overland Park, Lawrence

Major land areas: Central Plains, Great Plains, Ozark Plateau

Lowest point: Along the Verdigris River in Montgomery County, 679 feet (207 m) above sea level

Highest point: Mount Sunflower, 4,039 feet (1,231 m)

Major rivers: Arkansas River, Cimarron River, Kansas River, Missouri River, Republican River, Saline River, Smoky Hill River, Solomon River

Major bodies of water: Cheney Reservoir, John Redmond Reservoir, Kirwin Reservoir, Milford Lake, Perry Lake, Waconda Lake, Wilson Lake

Climate: In January the average temperature in Kansas is 32°F (0°C) and in July, 79°F (26°C). The average yearly precipitation is 40 inches (102 cm) in the southeastern part of the state and 17 inches (43 cm) in the western regions.

Resources, industries, and products: Transportation equipment, real estate, services, farm machinery, printing and publishing, cattle, hogs, wheat, corn, hay, sunflowers

History: Spanish explorers came to Kansas in the sixteenth century. France then claimed the territory in the late seventeenth century. In 1803 France sold the area to the United States as part of the Louisiana Purchase. The United States gave the land to eastern Indian tribes in 1825 and opened it up for settlers in 1854. In 1861 Kansas became the thirty-fourth state.

Historic sites and other attractions: Dwight D. Eisenhower's boyhood home in Abilene, Dodge City-Boot Hill and Frontier town, John Brown Memorial State Park, Hollenberg Pony Express Station, U.S. Cavalry Museum, Agricultural Hall of Fame and National Center, Kansas Cosmosphere and Space Discovery Center in Hutchinson

Unusual facts: Kansas is the leading producer of wheat in the nation. "Home on the Range" is the state song of Kansas. Dodge City, Kansas, was once called the Cowboy Capital of the World. The largest hailstone on record—weighing more than $1\frac{1}{2}$ pounds (680 g)—fell in Kansas.

Original American Indian groups: Kansa, Kiowa, Kiowa Apache

Harcourt Brace School Publishers

Name _____

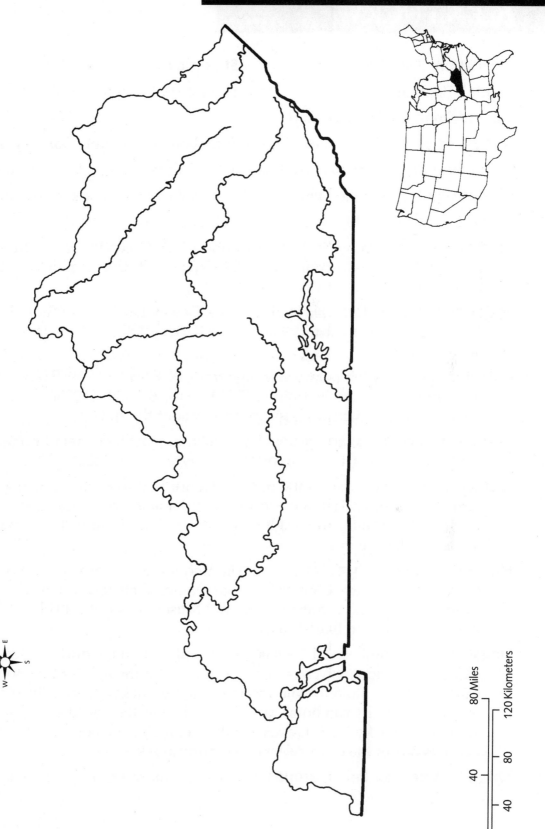

N E W S

Harcourt Brace School Publishers

80 Miles

120 Kilometers

40

80

40

0

0

FACTS ABOUT
KENTUCKY

Population: 3,908,000

Capital: Frankfort

State nickname: Bluegrass State

State flower: Goldenrod

State bird: Cardinal

Largest cities: Louisville, Lexington, Owensboro, Covington, Bowling Green

Major land areas: Appalachian Plateau, Gulf Coastal Plain, Interior Low Plateau

Lowest point: Along the Mississippi River, 257 feet (78 m) above sea level

Highest point: Black Mountain, 4,145 feet (1,264 m)

Major rivers: Big Sandy River, Cumberland River, Green River, Kentucky River, Licking River, Mississippi River, Ohio River, Salt River, Tennessee River, Tug Fork River

Major bodies of water: Dale Hollow Lake, Dewey Lake, Green River Lake, Herrington Lake, Kentucky Lake, Lake Barkley, Lake Cumberland (all artificial)

Climate: In January temperatures range from 22°F (-6°C) to 39°F (4°C), and in July temperatures range from 66°F (19°C) to 86°F (30°C). The average yearly precipitation is 45 inches (114 cm) throughout the state.

Resources, industries, and products: Industrial machinery, retail trade, electronics, horses, tobacco, corn, coal, soybeans, chickens

History: During the seventeenth and eighteenth centuries, the French and English came to Kentucky. The first European settlement was established there in 1774. In 1775 Daniel Boone led other settlers into the area. Kentucky became the fifteenth state in 1792.

Historic sites and other attractions: Mammoth Cave National Park, Abraham Lincoln's birthplace, Cumberland Gap National Historical Park, the Kentucky Derby, John James Audubon Memorial Museum, Natural Bridge, My Old Kentucky Home in Bardstown

Unusual facts: Cumberland Falls is the only place in the world outside of Africa that gets the moonbow, a rainbow formed from the light of the moon. Fort Knox holds the nation's gold reserve. The Kentucky Derby is the nation's oldest continually run horse race. Kentucky has the world's largest cave system. Kentucky Lake, created by the Kentucky Dam on the Tennessee River, is one of the country's largest artificial lakes.

Original American Indian groups: Cherokee, Chickawa, Shawnee, Yuchi

Harcourt Brace School Publishers

THE MAP BOOK

Name _____

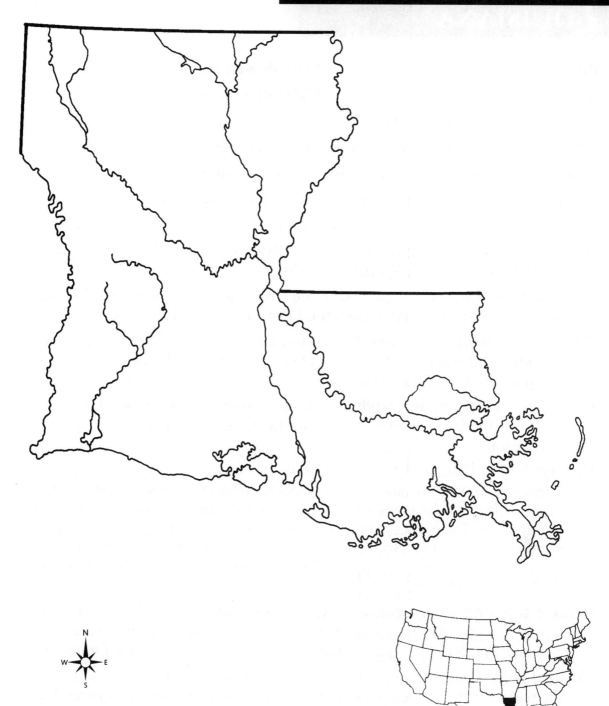

Harcourt Brace School Publishers

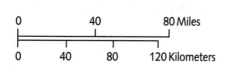

Name _____

LOUISIANA

Population: 4,351,000

Capital: Baton Rouge

State nickname: Pelican State

State flower: Magnolia

State bird: Eastern brown pelican

Largest cities: New Orleans, Baton Rouge, Shreveport, Metairie, Lafayette

Major land areas: Gulf Coastal Plain, Mississippi Alluvial Plain

Lowest point: In New Orleans, 8 feet (2.4 m) below sea level

Highest point: Driskill Mountain, 535 feet (163 m)

Major rivers: Atchafalaya River, Calcasieu River, Mississippi River, Ouachita River, Pearl River, Red River, Sabine River

Major bodies of water: Bayou d'Arbonne Lake, Calcasieu Lake, Grand Lake, Lake Maurepas, Lake Pontchartrain, Lake Salvador, White Lake

Climate: In January temperatures range from 42°F (6°C) to 61°F (16°C), and in July temperatures range from 73°F (23°C) to 91°F (33°C). The average yearly precipitation is 62 inches (157 cm).

Resources, industries, and products: Trade, tourism, fishing, mining, petroleum products, lumber, transportation equipment, rice, sugarcane, sweet potatoes, salt, cotton

History: In 1528 Cabeza de Vaca and Pánfilo de Narváez became the first Europeans to visit the area. In 1682 Robert La Salle claimed the Mississippi River valley area for France. In 1699 the royal French colony of Louisiana was founded. In 1762 France transferred the region to Spain. Spain in turn gave it back to France in 1800. In 1803 the United States purchased the Louisiana Territory from France for about $15 million, in the Louisiana Purchase. In 1812 Louisiana became the eighteenth state.

Historic sites and other attractions: Chalmette National Historical Park, Avery Island, Longfellow-Evangeline Memorial Park, French Quarter in New Orleans, Mardi Gras, Aquarium of the Americas, Battle of New Orleans site

Unusual facts: Louisiana ranks second to Texas in mineral production and leads the nation in the production of hardwoods (oak, gum, hickory, cypress). The world's longest bridge is the Lake Pontchartrain Causeway, which extends 29 miles (47 km). The Superdome in New Orleans is the largest indoor stadium in the world. More goods go in and out of the port of New Orleans than any other port in the country.

Original American Indian groups: Acolapissa, Apalachee, Atalapa, Avoyel, Bayogoula, Chitimacha, Natchitoches, Tunica

Harcourt Brace School Publishers

THE MAP BOOK

Name _____

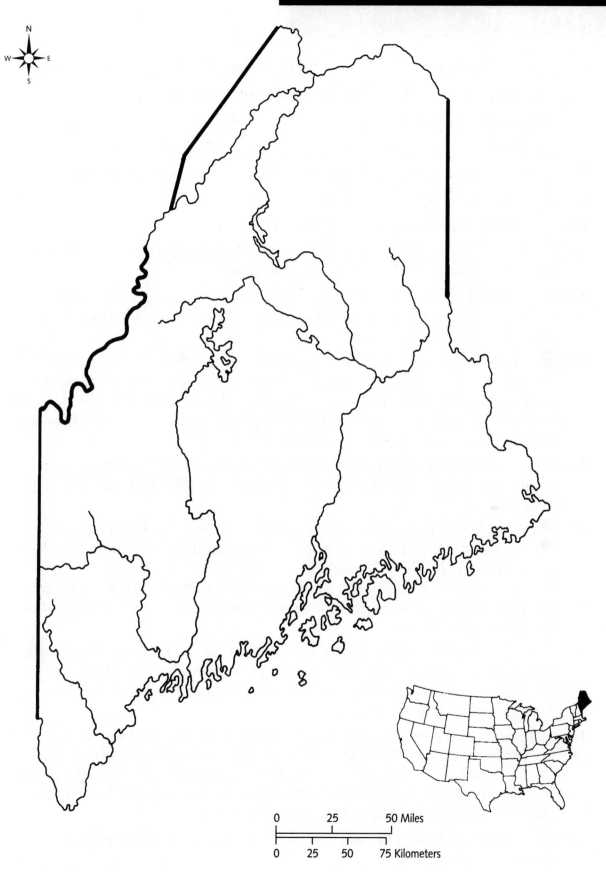

N
W   E
S

Harcourt Brace School Publishers

0   25   50 Miles

0   25   50   75 Kilometers

Name _____

FACTS ABOUT

MAINE

Population: 1,242,000

Capital: Augusta

State nickname: Pine Tree State

Largest cities: Portland, Lewiston, Bangor, Auburn, South Portland

Major land areas: Coastal Lowlands, New England Upland, White Mountains

Lowest point: Along the coast, sea level

Highest point: Mount Katahdin, 5,268 feet (1,606 m)

Major rivers: Allagash River, Androscoggin River, Kennebec River, Penobscot River, Saco River, St. Croix River, St. John River

Major bodies of water: Chamberlain Lake, Chesuncook Lake, Eagle Lake (artificial), Flagstaff Lake, Grand Lake, Moosehead Lake, Penobscot Bay, Rangeley Lake, Sebago Lake

Climate: In the north temperatures range from -2°F (-19°C) to 19°F (-7°C) in January and from 55°F (13°C) to 77°F (25°C) in July. In the south temperatures range from 11°F (-12°C) to 30°F (-1°C) in January and from 58°F (14°C) to 79°F (26°C) in July. The average yearly precipitation is 37 inches (94 cm) in the north and 44 inches (112 cm) in the south.

Resources, industries, and products: Fishing, paper products, transportation equipment, lumber and wood products, potatoes, apples, blueberries, hay, chickens

History: French explorers reached Maine in the sixteenth century. English colonists first settled in Maine in 1607. They established permanent settlements in the 1620s. In 1622 England gave the land to Ferdinando Gorges. His descendants sold Maine to Massachusetts for about $6,000. Hundreds of Maine patriots fought in the American Revolution. In 1820 Maine became the twenty-third state.

Historic sites and other attractions: Acadia National Park, Henry Wadsworth Longfellow House, Burnham Tavern, Old Gaol Museum, Fort Popham Memorial, Penobscot Marine Museum, Fort Western, Seashore Trolley Museum, Sugarloaf ski area

Unusual facts: The Portland Head Light, built in 1791, is one of the oldest lighthouses in the nation. West Quoddy Head is the easternmost point in the United States. Almost nine-tenths of Maine is covered by forests. The 2,000 islands off Maine's coast are really the tops of old mountains. More toothpicks are produced in Maine than in any other state.

Original American Indian groups: Abenaki, Malecite, Passamaquoddy, Pennacook, Penobscot

State flower: White pine cone and tassel

State bird: Chickadee

Harcourt Brace School Publishers

Name _____

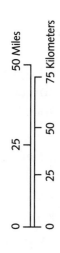

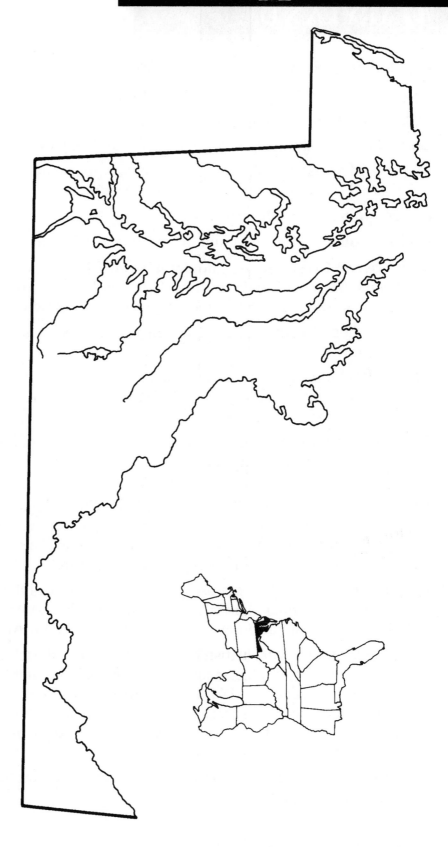

Harcourt Brace School Publishers

THE MAP BOOK

Name _____

FACTS ABOUT
MARYLAND

Population: 5,094,000

Capital: Annapolis

State flower: Black-eyed Susan

State bird: Baltimore oriole

State nicknames: Old Line State, Free State

Largest cities: Baltimore, Silver Spring, Columbia, Dundalk, Bethesda

Major land areas: Appalachian Mountains, Appalachian Plateau, Atlantic Coastal Plain, Blue Ridge Mountains, Piedmont

Lowest point: Along the ocean, sea level

Highest point: Backbone Mountain, 3,360 feet (1,024 m)

Major rivers: Chester River, Choptank River, Elk River, Gunpowder River, Nanticoke River, Patapsco River, Patuxent River, Pocomoke River, Potomac River, Sassafras River, Susquehanna River, Wicomico River

Major bodies of water: Chesapeake Bay, Deep Creek Lake (artificial), Liberty Lake (artificial)

Climate: In January temperatures range from 23°F (-5°C) to 40°F (4°C), and in July temperatures range from 67°F (19°C) to 87°F (31°C). The average yearly precipitation is 41 inches (104 cm).

Resources, industries, and products: Biotechnology and information technology, electronics, electrical machinery, chemicals, fishing, tourism, food products, stone, chickens, oysters, corn, soybeans

History: In 1608 Captain John Smith explored Chesapeake Bay. The first English settlers arrived in 1634. In 1649 Maryland passed a religious toleration act giving equal rights to all Christians. In 1776 Maryland declared its independence. In 1788 Maryland became the seventh state.

Historic sites and other attractions: Antietam National Battlefield Site, Fort McHenry National Monument, United States Naval Academy, Peale Museum, Clara Barton National Historic Site, Edgar Allan Poe House

Unusual facts: After the British bombardment of Fort McHenry in 1814, Francis Scott Key wrote "The Star-Spangled Banner." The first telegraph line in the nation was opened in 1844. The state capitol in Annapolis is the oldest statehouse still in use. The first American coal-burning steam locomotive was tested in Maryland in 1830. Maryland is the leading producer of oysters in the United States.

Original American Indian groups: Conoy, Delaware, Nanticoke, Powhatan, Shawnee, Susquehanna

Harcourt Brace School Publishers

THE MAP BOOK

Name _____

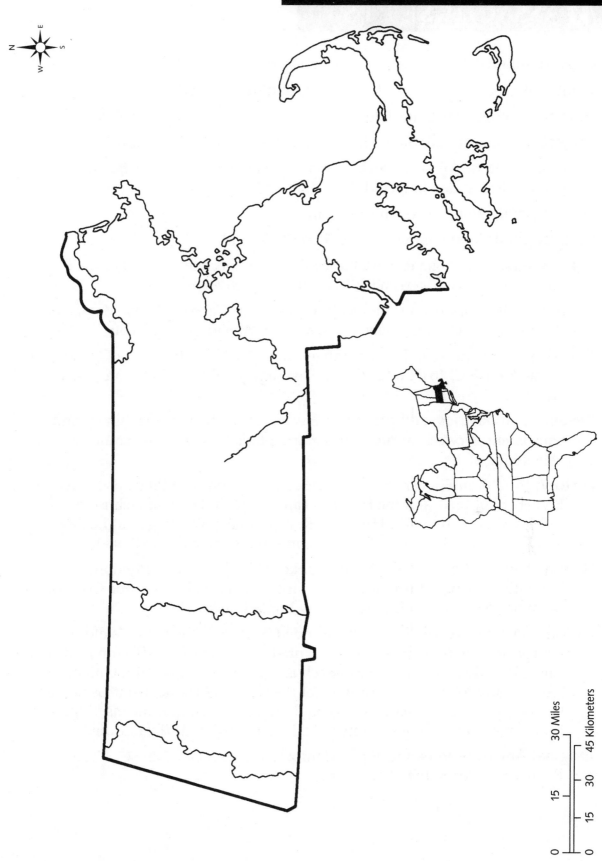

Harcourt Brace School Publishers

30 Miles

45 Kilometers

Name _____

FACTS ABOUT
MASSACHUSETTS

Population: 6,118,000

Capital: Boston

State nicknames: Bay State, Old Colony

State flower: Mayflower

State bird: Chickadee

Largest cities: Boston, Worcester, Springfield, Lowell, New Bedford

Major land areas: Appalachian Mountains, Berkshire Hills, Coastal Lowlands, Connecticut Valley Lowland, New England Upland

Lowest point: Along the Atlantic Ocean, sea level

Highest point: Mount Greylock, 3,491 feet (1,064 m)

Major rivers: Blackstone River, Charles River, Connecticut River, Hoosic River, Housatonic River, Merrimack River, Taunton River

Major bodies of water: Boston Bay, Buzzards Bay, Cape Cod Bay, Massachusetts Bay, Nantucket Sound, Quabbin Reservoir, Wachusett Reservoir

Climate: Temperatures in January range from 22°F (-6°C) to 36°F (2°C) and in July from 65°F (18°C) to 82°F (28°C). The average yearly precipitation is 42 inches (107 cm).

Resources, industries, and products: Electronics, industrial machinery and equipment, services, trade, printing and publishing, fishing, cranberries, vegetables, stone

History: In 1602 an English explorer visited the region. The Pilgrims landed at Plymouth in 1620, and the Puritans came in 1630. The Massachusetts Bay Colony was chartered in 1691. The Revolutionary War began at Lexington and Concord in 1775. In 1788 Massachusetts became the sixth state.

Historic sites and other attractions: Bunker Hill Monument, Plymouth Plantation, John and Priscilla Alden House, Walden Pond, Cape Cod National Seashore, Museum of Fine Arts, New England Aquarium

Unusual facts: Harvard University, founded in 1636, is the nation's oldest college. Alexander Graham Bell invented the telephone in Boston in 1876. Three Presidents were from Massachusetts: John Adams, John Quincy Adams, and John F. Kennedy. One of the lakes in Massachusetts is named Chargoggagoggmanchaugagoggchaubunagungamaug. It means "You fish on your side and I'll fish on my side. Nobody fishes in the middle."

Original American Indian groups: Mahican, Massachuset, Nauset, Nipmuc, Pennacook, Pocomtuc, Wampanoag

Harcourt Brace School Publishers

THE MAP BOOK

Name _____

Harcourt Brace School Publishers

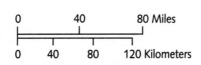

Name _____

FACTS ABOUT
MICHIGAN

Population: 9,773,000   **State flower:** Apple blossom

Capital: Lansing   **State bird:** Robin

State nicknames: Wolverine State, Great Lakes State

Largest cities: Detroit, Grand Rapids, Warren, Flint, Lansing, Ann Arbor

Major land areas: Central Plains, Superior Upland

Lowest point: Along Lake Erie, 571 feet (174 m) above sea level

Highest point: Mount Arvon, 1,979 feet (603 m)

Major rivers: Detroit River, Escanaba River, Grand River, Kalamazoo River, Menominee River, Muskegon River, Saint Clair River

Major bodies of water: Grand Traverse Bay, Green Bay, Houghton Lake, Lake Erie, Lake Gogebic, Lake Huron, Lake Michigan, Lake Saint Clair, Lake Superior, Saginaw Bay, Straits of Mackinac, Upper and Lower Tahquamenon Falls, Whitefish Bay

Climate: In January temperatures range from 5°F (-15°C) to 21°F (-6°C) in the Upper Peninsula and from 16°F (-9°C) to 30°F (-1°C) in the Lower Peninsula. In July temperatures range from 51°F (11°C) to 76°F (24°C) in the Upper Peninsula and from 61°F (16°C) to 83°F (28°C) in the Lower Peninsula. The average yearly precipitation is 33 inches (84 cm) throughout the state.

Resources, industries, and products: Automobiles, buses, trucks, mining, plastics, office furniture, winter wheat, fishing, iron ore, cherries, corn, honey, salt

History: During the seventeenth century, the French explored and settled in the Michigan region. In 1763 the British took possession of the region after defeating the French in the French and Indian War. In 1787 Michigan was added to the Northwest Territory of the United States. It was later established as the Territory of Michigan in 1805. In 1837 Michigan became the twenty-sixth state.

Historic sites and other attractions: Greenfield Village, Henry Ford Museum, Isle Royale National Park, the Soo Canals, Warren Dunes State Park, Michigan Space Center, Pictured Rocks, Tahquamenon Falls

Unusual facts: Michigan is the leading producer of automobiles in the nation. Battle Creek produces more breakfast cereal than any other city in the world. One of the nation's largest salt mines lies about 1,000 feet (300 m) under Detroit.

Original American Indian groups: Chippewa, Menominee, Miami, Neutrals, Ottawa, Potawatomi

Harcourt Brace School Publishers

Name _____

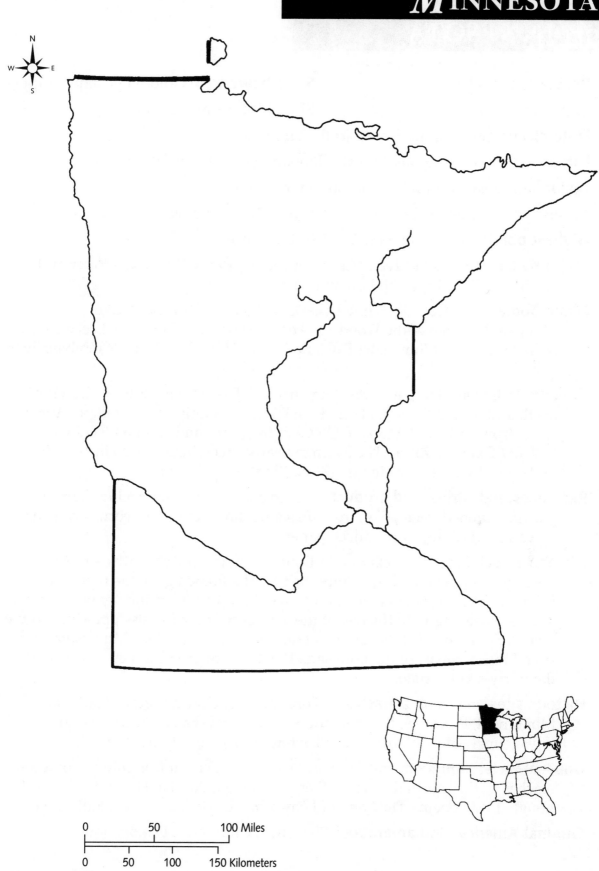

N
W E
S

Harcourt Brace School Publishers

0   50   100 Miles

0   50   100   150 Kilometers

Name _____

Population: 4,685,000

Capital: St. Paul

State flower: Pink and white lady's slipper

State bird: Common loon

State nicknames: Gopher State, North Star State

Largest cities: Minneapolis, St. Paul, Bloomington, Duluth, Rochester

Major land areas: Central Plains, Superior Upland

Lowest point: Along Lake Superior, 600 feet (183 m) above sea level

Highest point: Eagle Mountain, 2,301 feet (701 m)

Major rivers: Minnesota River, Mississippi River, Rainy River, Red River of the North, St. Croix River, St. Louis River

Major bodies of water: Big Stone Lake, Cass Lake, Lake Itasca, Lake Minnetonka, Lake of the Woods, Lake Superior, Lake Traverse, Leech Lake, Mille Lacs Lake, Minnehaha Falls, Red Lake, Vermilion Lake, Winnibigoshish Lake

Climate: In January temperatures range from -2°F (-19°C) to 16°F (-9°C) in the north and from 3°F (-16°C) to 21°F (-6°C) in the south. In July temperatures range from 55°F (13°C) to 77°F (25°C) in the north and from 63°F (17°C) to 84°F (29°C) in the south. The average yearly precipitation is 30 inches (76 cm) in the northwest and 28 inches (71 cm) in the southeast.

Resources, industries, and products: Office and computing machines, meat packing, canned vegetables, iron ore, cattle, hogs, chickens, corn, soybeans, wheat, tourism, forest products, paper

History: French fur traders explored Minnesota in the seventeenth century, and the region was claimed by France. In 1763 the French gave the region to Britain after losing the French and Indian War. In 1783 Britain gave eastern Minnesota, along with the rest of the land east of the Mississippi River, to the United States. In 1803 the United States bought the western Minnesota area from France as part of the Louisiana Purchase. In 1858 Minnesota became the thirty-second state.

Historic sites and other attractions: Fort Snelling, Grand Portage National Monument, Pipestone National Monument, High Falls, Guthrie Theater, Voyageurs National Park, St. Paul Winter Carnival, Minnehaha Falls

Unusual facts: Minnesota has the world's largest open-pit iron mine. Minnesota reaches farther north than any other state except Alaska. Henry Wadsworth Longfellow's poem "The Song of Hiawatha" made Minnehaha Falls famous.

Original American Indian groups: Cheyenne, Chippewa, Dakota, Iowa

Harcourt Brace School Publishers

Name _____

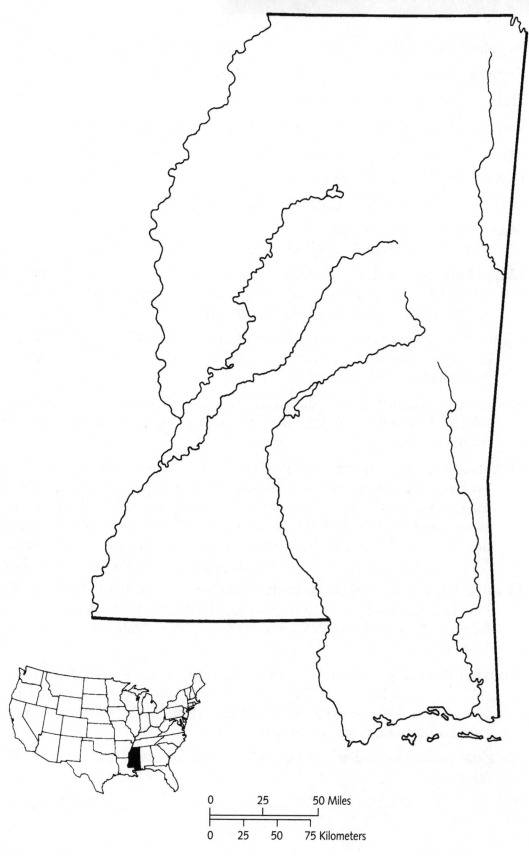

0   25   50 Miles

0   25   50   75 Kilometers

Name _____

MISSISSIPPI

Population: 2,730,000

State flower: Magnolia

Capital: Jackson

State bird: Mockingbird

State nickname: Magnolia State

Largest cities: Jackson, Biloxi, Greenville, Hattiesburg, Meridian

Major land areas: Gulf Coastal Plain, Mississippi Alluvial Plain

Lowest point: Gulf of Mexico, sea level

Highest point: Woodall Mountain, 806 feet (246 m)

Major rivers: Big Black River, Chickasawhay River, Mississippi River, Pascagoula River, Pearl River, Tombigbee River, Yazoo River

Major bodies of water: Arkabutla Lake (artificial), Enid Lake, Grenada Lake (artificial), Gulf of Mexico, Mississippi Sound, Pickwick Lake (artificial), Ross Barnett Reservoir, Sardis Lake (artificial)

Climate: In January temperatures range from 33°F (1°C) to 56°F (13°C), and in July temperatures range from 71°F (22°C) to 92°F (33°C). The average yearly precipitation is 55 inches (140 cm).

Resources, industries, and products: Trade, lumber and wood products, electrical machinery, food products, fishing, soybeans, cotton, rice, catfish, chickens, stone

History: In 1540 Spanish explorers searched the region for gold. In 1682 a French explorer claimed the entire Mississippi River valley for France. This area included present-day Mississippi. The first European settlement was established in 1699. In 1763 the British took possession of the region after defeating the French in the French and Indian War. In 1798 the Mississippi Territory was formed. In 1817 Mississippi became the twentieth state.

Historic sites and other attractions: The Old Capitol State Historical Museum, Fort Massachusetts, Vicksburg National Military Park, Petrified Forest, Jefferson Davis's home at Biloxi, mansions near Natchez, Florewood River Plantation

Unusual facts: The Petrified Forest contains giant stone trees dating back 30 million years. The word *Mississippi*, used by Indians to describe the Mississippi River, means "great water." Mississippi has over 4,700 tree farms—more than any other state.

Original American Indian groups: Biloxi, Chickasaw, Choctaw, Natchez, Tunica, Yazoo

Harcourt Brace School Publishers

Name _____

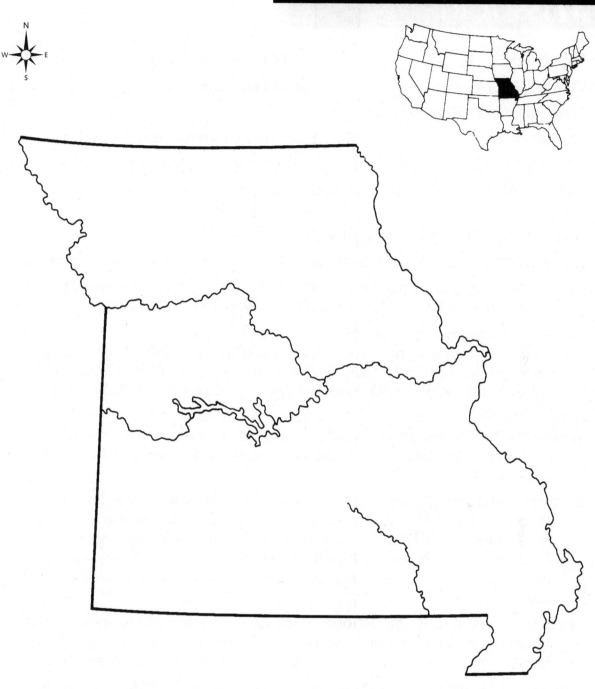

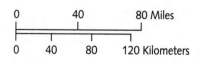

0   40   80 Miles

0   40   80   120 Kilometers

FACTS ABOUT
MISSOURI

Population: 5,402,000

Capital: Jefferson City

State nickname: Show Me State

State flower: Hawthorn

State bird: Bluebird

Largest cities: Kansas City, St. Louis, Springfield, Independence, St. Joseph

Major land areas: Central Plains, Mississippi Alluvial Plain, Ozark Plateau

Lowest point: Along the St. Francis River, near Cardwell, 230 feet (70 m) above sea level

Highest point: Taum Sauk Mountain, 1,772 feet (540 m)

Major rivers: Current River, Mississippi River, Missouri River, Osage River

Major bodies of water: Bull Shoals Lake, Lake of the Ozarks, Pomme de Terre Lake, Table Rock Lake, Taneycomo Lake, Wappapello Reservoir (all artificial)

Climate: In January temperatures range from 17°F (-8°C) to 35°F (2°C) in the north and from 21°F (-6°C) to 38°F (3°C) in the southeast. In July temperatures range from 68°F (20°C) to 89°F (32°C) in the north and from 70°F (21°C) to 89°F (32°C) in the southeast. The average yearly precipitation is 38 inches (97 cm) throughout the state.

Resources, industries, and products: Aerospace, tourism, transportation equipment, food products, electronics, chemicals, soybeans, corn, turkeys, chickens, lead

History: In the seventeenth century, French explorers claimed Missouri for France. About 1735, the first permanent European settlement was founded in Ste. Genevieve. In 1762 France gave the region to Spain. The region was returned to France in 1800. In 1803 the United States bought the region as part of the Louisiana Purchase. In 1821 Missouri became the twenty-fourth state.

Historic sites and other attractions: Mark Twain Home and Museum, George Washington Carver National Monument, Harry S. Truman Library, Pony Express Museum, Winston Churchill Memorial and Library, Branson

Unusual facts: Independence was the starting point for both the Oregon and Santa Fe trails. For this reason, Missouri is sometimes called Mother of the West. Missouri is one of two states that are bordered by eight states. (The other is Tennessee.) Gateway Arch in St. Louis, completed in 1965 and made of stainless steel, is the world's tallest monument. It is 630 feet (192 m) high. Missouri produces more lead than any other state.

Original American Indian groups: Fox, Missouri, Osage, Sauk

THE MAP BOOK

Name _____

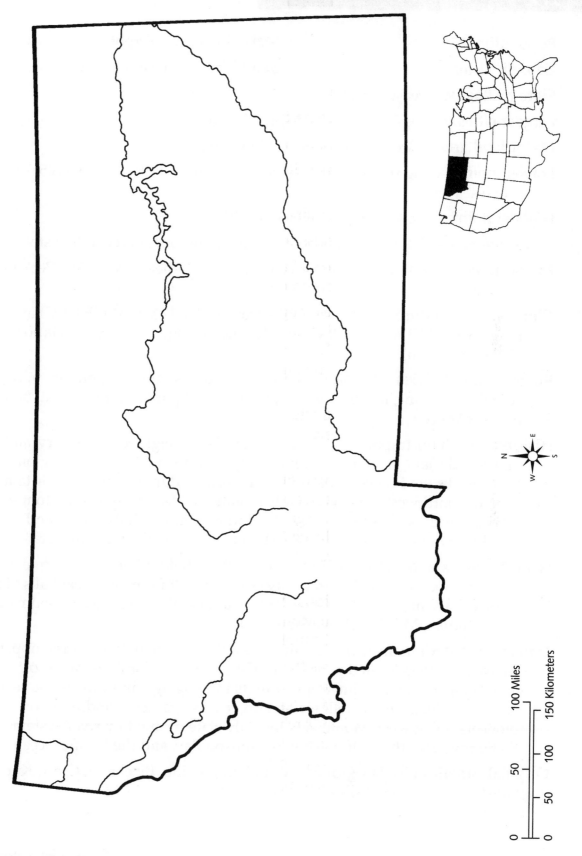

Harcourt Brace School Publishers

100 Miles

150 Kilometers

50   100

50   100

0   0

FACTS ABOUT
MONTANA

Population: 878,000

Capital: Helena

State nickname: Treasure State

Largest cities: Billings, Great Falls, Missoula, Butte, Helena

Major land areas: Great Plains, Rocky Mountains

Lowest point: Along the Kootenai River in Lincoln County, 1,800 feet (549 m) above sea level

Highest point: Granite Peak, 12,799 feet (3,901 m)

Major rivers: Clark Fork River, Kootenai River, Missouri River, Yellowstone River

Major bodies of water: Canyon Ferry Reservoir, Flathead Lake, Fort Peck Lake (artificial)

State flower: Bitterroot

State bird: Western meadowlark

Climate: Temperatures in January range from 10°F (-12°C) to 30°F (-1°C) and from 53°F (12°C) to 85°F (29°C) in July. The average yearly precipitation is 12 inches (30 cm).

Resources, industries, and products: Food products, mining, petroleum, coal, copper, gold, zinc, tourism, wood products and paper, cattle, wheat, barley, hay, sugar beets

History: French fur trappers reached Montana in the eighteenth century, and Lewis and Clark passed through the region in 1805. Most of the region was purchased from France as part of the Louisiana Purchase in 1803. Britain gave the northwest part to the United States in 1846. In 1864 the Montana Territory was established. In 1877 the Indian wars with the Sioux and Nez Perce Indians ended. In 1889 Montana became the forty-first state.

Historic sites and other attractions: Custer Battlefield National Monument, Glacier National Park, Virginia City, Medicine Monument, Great Falls of the Missouri, Giant Springs at Great Falls, National Bison Range, Museum of the Plains Indian, Morrison Cave State Park

Unusual facts: Montana is the fourth-largest state in the nation. Grasshopper Glacier, which is located near Cooke City, is named for the swarms of grasshoppers that became trapped in its ice long ago and can still be seen. Pompey's Pillar on the Yellowstone River was a famous landmark for pioneers going west. Montana is the only state drained by river systems that empty into the Gulf of Mexico, Hudson Bay, and the Pacific Ocean.

Original American Indian groups: Assiniboin, Atsina, Blackfoot, Crow, Kutenai, Salish

Harcourt Brace School Publishers

THE MAP BOOK

NEBRASKA

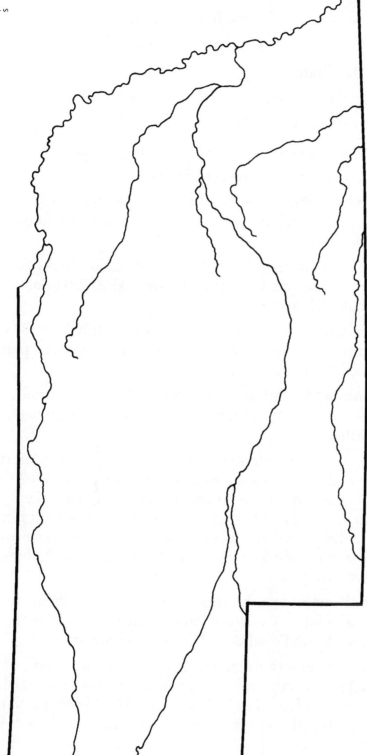

80 Miles

120 Kilometers

80

80

40

40

0

0

FACTS ABOUT
NEBRASKA

Population: 1,656,000

Capital: Lincoln

State flower: Goldenrod

State bird: Western meadowlark

State nickname: Cornhusker State

Largest cities: Omaha, Lincoln, Grand Island, Bellevue, Kearney, Fremont

Major land areas: Central Plains, Great Plains

Lowest point: In Richardson County, 840 feet (256 m) above sea level

Highest point: In Kimball County, 5,426 feet (1,654 m)

Major rivers: Big Blue River, Elkhorn River, Little Blue River, Loup River, Missouri River, Niobrara River, North Platte River, Platte River, Republican River, South Platte River

Major bodies of water: Enders Reservoir, Harlan County Lake, Harry Strunk Lake, Jeffrey Reservoir, Johnson Lake, Lake McConaughy, Sutherland Reservoir, Swanson Lake (all artificial)

Climate: In January temperatures average 23°F (-5°C) and in July 76°F (24°C). The average precipitation ranges from 15 inches (38 cm) in the western part of the state to 30 inches (76 cm) in the eastern part.

Resources, industries, and products: Processed foods, electronics, meat packing, dairy products, transportation equipment, corn, soybeans, hay, wheat, potatoes, chickens, cattle, flour

History: During the seventeenth and eighteenth centuries, French explorers and trappers traveled through Nebraska on their way to Oregon. In 1762 France gave Nebraska to Spain as part of the Louisiana Territory. Spain then returned Nebraska to France in 1800, and the United States bought it in the Louisiana Purchase of 1803. Settlement began in the Nebraska Territory in 1854. When Congress passed the Kansas-Nebraska Act in 1867, Nebraska became the thirty-seventh state.

Historic sites and other attractions: Arbor Lodge, Scouts Rest Ranch, Stuhr Museum of the Prairie Pioneer, Toadstool Park, Homestead National Monument of America, Agate Fossil Beds National Monument

Unusual facts: The largest mammoth fossil ever found was unearthed in 1922 near North Platte. Nebraska is the only state with a single-house legislature. The first Arbor Day was celebrated in Nebraska in 1872. Nebraska National Forest and McKelvie National Forest are the only two national forests planted entirely by foresters.

Original American Indian groups: Arapaho, Cheyenne, Omaha, Oto, Pawnee, Ponca

THE MAP BOOK

Name _____

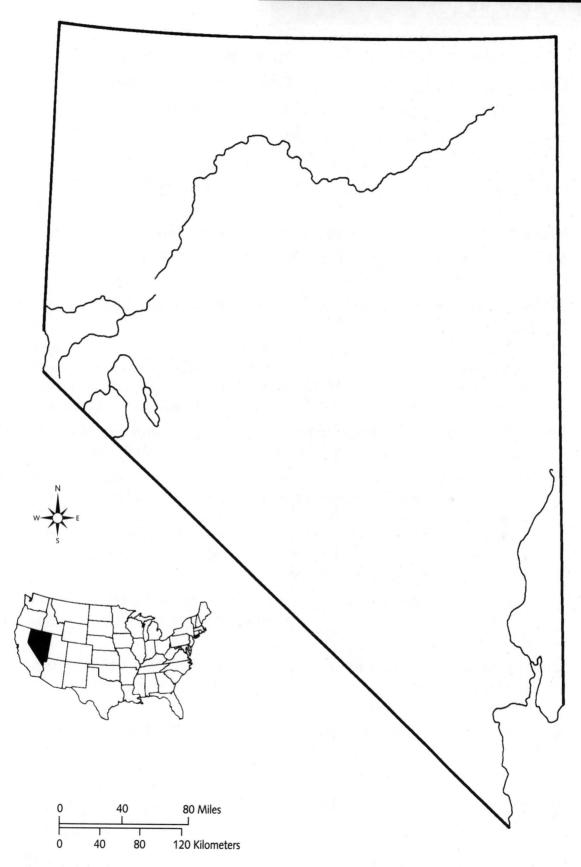

N
W — E
S

```
0        40        80 Miles
0    40      80   120 Kilometers
```

Name _____

Population: 1,676,000

State flower: Sagebrush

Capital: Carson City

State bird: Mountain bluebird

State nicknames: Silver State, Sagebrush State, Battle Born State

Largest cities: Las Vegas, Reno, Henderson, Sparks, Carson City, Elko

Major land areas: Basin and Range Region, Columbia Plateau, Sierra Nevada

Lowest point: Along the Colorado River in Clark County, 470 feet (143 m) above sea level

Highest point: Boundary Peak in Esmeralda County, 13,140 feet (4,005 m)

Major rivers: Carson River, Colorado River, Humboldt River, Meadow Valley Wash, Truckee River, Walker River

Major bodies of water: Franklin Lake, Lake Mead (artificial), Lake Tahoe, Pyramid Lake, Ruby Lake, Walker Lake

Climate: In January temperatures range from 21 °F (-6 °C) to 45 °F (7 °C), and in July temperatures range from 51 °F (11 °C) to 92 °F (33 °C). The average yearly precipitation ranges from 0 to 24 inches (61 cm) in various parts of the state. The rainiest parts of Nevada are in the Sierra Nevada and their eastern foothills.

Resources, industries, and products: Gaming, tourism, mining, chemicals, lawn and garden irrigation equipment, hay, onions, garlic, alfalfa seeds, gold, silver

History: A Spanish missionary who was traveling from New Mexico to California was probably the first European to enter the Nevada region, in 1776. Fur traders and trappers explored the Nevada area in the early 1800s. In 1848 the United States won the territory from Mexico. In 1859 silver was discovered near Virginia City. Nevada Territory was created in 1861, and the region became the thirty-sixth state in 1864.

Historic sites and other attractions: Humboldt National Forest, Lehman Caves National Monument, Valley of Fire, Rhyolite, Geyser Basin, Lake Tahoe State Park, Hoover Dam

Unusual facts: Nevada has less rainfall than any other state. Ruth Copper Pit is one of the largest open-pit copper mines in the world. Hoover Dam is one of the world's largest dams.

Original American Indian groups: Paiute, Shoshoni, Washoe

Harcourt Brace School Publishers

Name _____

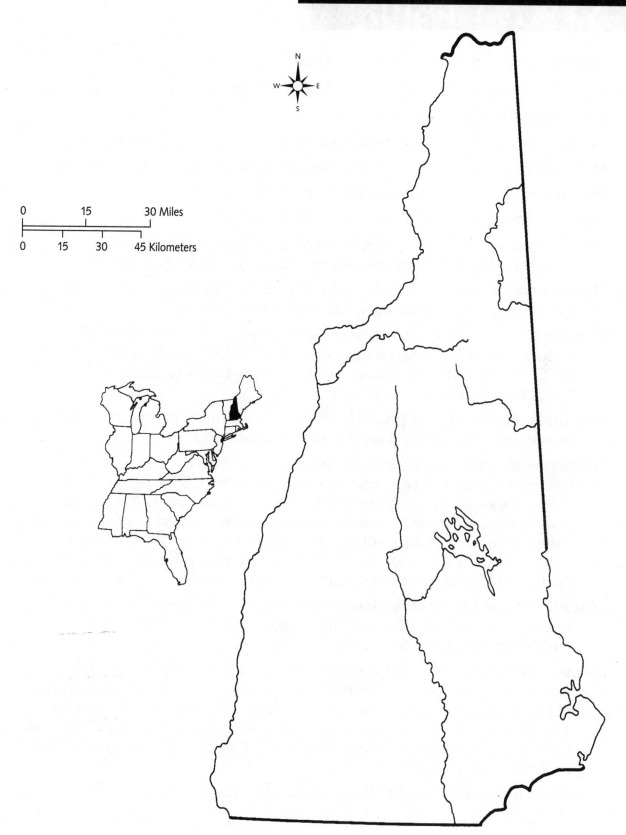

0   15   30 Miles

0   15   30   45 Kilometers

Harcourt Brace School Publishers

FACTS ABOUT
NEW HAMPSHIRE

Population: 1,172,000

Capital: Concord

State nickname: Granite State

State flower: Purple lilac

State bird: Purple finch

Largest cities: Manchester, Nashua, Concord, Rochester, Portsmouth

Major land areas: Coastal Lowlands, New England Upland, White Mountains

Lowest point: Along the Atlantic Ocean, sea level

Highest point: Mount Washington, 6,288 feet (1,917 m)

Major rivers: Ammonoosuc River, Androscoggin River, Connecticut River, Merrimack River, Pemigewasset River, Piscataqua River, Saco River

Major bodies of water: Great Bay, Lake Winnipesaukee, Ossipee Lake, Squam Lake, Sunapee Lake, Umbagog Lake, Winnisquam Lake

Climate: In January temperatures average 16°F (-9°C) in the north and 22°F (-6°C) in the south. In July temperatures average 66°F (19°C) in the north and 70°F (21°C) in the south. The average yearly precipitation is 42 inches (107 cm) throughout the state.

Resources, industries, and products: Tourism, electronics, mining, machinery, plastics, metal products, dairy products, maple syrup

History: In the early seventeenth century, English explorers came to New Hampshire, and the first permanent English settlement was established during the 1620s. New Hampshire Colony was chartered by King Charles II as a royal colony in 1680. New Hampshire was the first colony to declare its independence from Great Britain—six months before the Declaration of Independence was signed in 1776. In 1788 New Hampshire leaders signed the United States Constitution, and New Hampshire became the ninth state.

Historic sites and other attractions: White Mountain National Forest, Franklin Pierce Homestead at Hillsboro, Profile Mountain, Daniel Webster's birthplace, Strawberry Banke, Flume, Mount Washington

Unusual facts: The library in Peterborough, founded in 1833, is one of the oldest tax-supported public libraries in the nation. New Hampshire's House of Representatives, with 400 members, is larger than that of any other state. The strongest winds ever measured at the Earth's surface, 188 miles per hour (303 kph), struck Mount Washington in 1934. One gust of wind reached 231 miles per hour (372 kph).

Original American Indian groups: Abenaki, Pennacook

Harcourt Brace School Publishers

THE MAP BOOK

Name _____

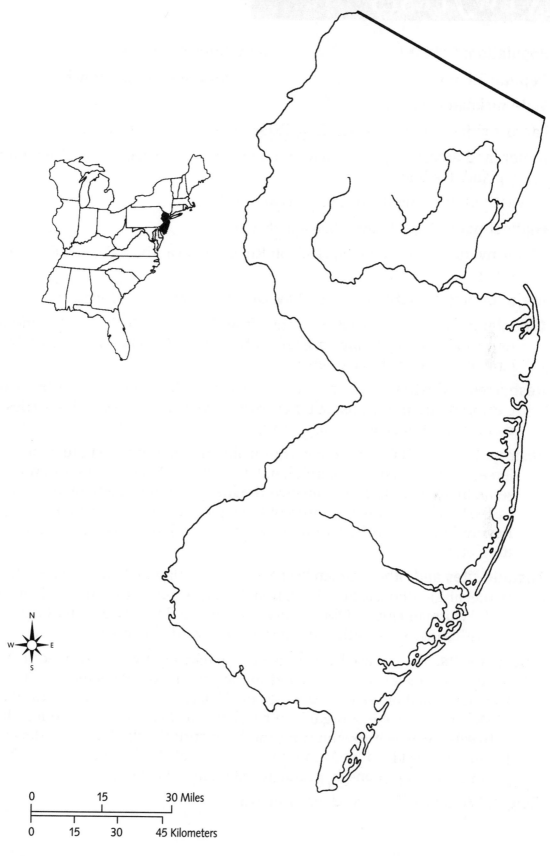

N
W — E
S

0   15   30 Miles
0   15   30   45 Kilometers

Harcourt Brace School Publishers

Name _____

FACTS ABOUT
NEW JERSEY

Population: 8,052,000

Capital: Trenton

State nickname: Garden State

State flower: Purple violet

State bird: Eastern goldfinch

Largest cities: Newark, Jersey City, Paterson, Elizabeth, Woodbridge

Major land areas: Appalachian Mountains, Atlantic Coastal Plain, New England Upland, Piedmont

Lowest point: Along the Atlantic Ocean, sea level

Highest point: High Point, 1,803 feet (550 m)

Major rivers: Delaware River, Hudson River, Mullica River, Passaic River, Raritan River

Major bodies of water: Barnegat Bay, Delaware Bay, Lake Hopatcong

Climate: In January temperatures range from 21°F (-6°C) to 40°F (4°C), and in July temperatures range from 65°F (18°C) to 85°F (29°C). The average yearly precipitation is 40 inches (102 cm).

Resources, industries, and products: Services, trade, chemicals, electrical and electronic equipment, fishing, hay, corn, soybeans, peppers, blueberries, cranberries, tomatoes

History: Giovanni da Verrazano was probably the first European to explore New Jersey, in 1524. People from Holland and Sweden were the first Europeans to settle there. The Dutch established the first permanent settlement in Bergen. In 1664 the English won control of the region. During the American Revolution, many battles were fought there. In 1787 New Jersey became the third state.

Historic sites and other attractions: Morristown National Historical Park, Barnegat Lighthouse, Edison National Historic Site, Princeton University, Walt Whitman House, Old Barracks in Trenton, Delaware Water Gap, Palisades Interstate Park, Atlantic City, Harvard University

Unusual facts: The electric light bulb and the telegraph were invented in New Jersey. New Jersey leads the states in the production of chemicals. Princeton was the capital of the United States in 1783, and Trenton was the capital in 1784. The first game of organized baseball was played in Hoboken in 1846 between the New York Nine and the New York Knickerbockers. Alexander Hamilton was killed by Aaron Burr in a duel at Weehawken in 1804. New Jersey is the most densely populated state in the nation.

Original American Indian group: Delaware

Harcourt Brace School Publishers

THE MAP BOOK

Name _____

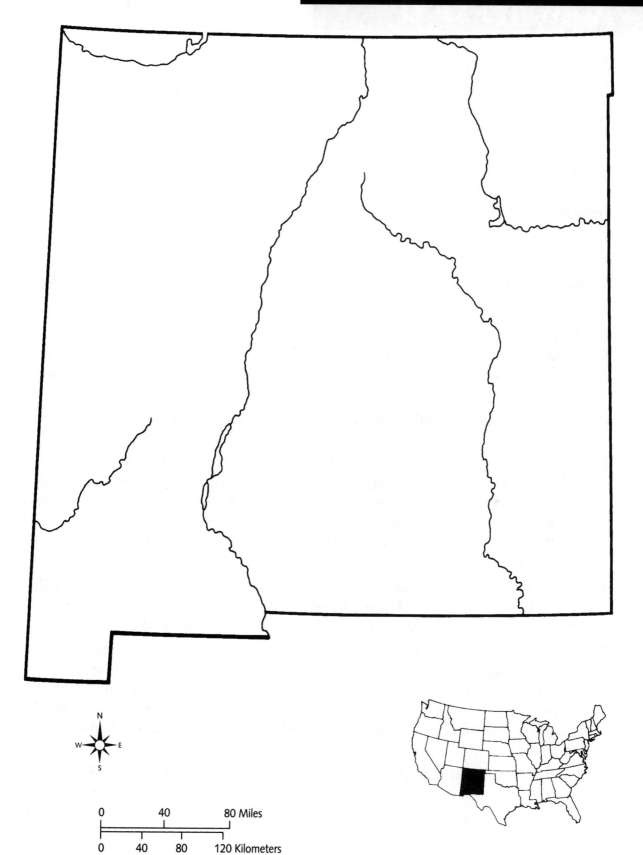

Harcourt Brace School Publishers

N
W • E
S

0   40   80 Miles

0   40   80   120 Kilometers

FACTS ABOUT
NEW MEXICO

Population: 1,729,000

Capital: Santa Fe

State nickname: Land of Enchantment

State flower: Yucca

State bird: Roadrunner

Largest cities: Albuquerque, Las Cruces, Santa Fe, Roswell, Rio Rancho

Major land areas: Basin and Range Region, Colorado Plateau, Great Plains, Rocky Mountains

Lowest point: Red Bluff Reservoir in Eddy County, 2,817 feet (859 m) above sea level

Highest point: Wheeler Peak in Taos County, 13,161 feet (4,011 m)

Major rivers: Canadian River, Gila River, Pecos River, Rio Grande, San Juan River

Major bodies of water: Conchas Reservoir, Elephant Butte Reservoir, Navajo Reservoir

Climate: In January temperatures range from 22°F (-6°C) to 47°F (8°C), and in July temperatures range from 64°F (18°C) to 93°F (34°C). The average yearly precipitation is 9 inches (23 cm).

Resources, industries, and products: Machinery, lumber, transportation equipment, hay, onions, wheat, pecans, cotton, sorghum, cattle, copper, potash

History: During the sixteenth century, Spanish explorers searched New Mexico for gold. Spain claimed the territory, and settlements were established there in 1598. In 1821 Spain surrendered the territory to Mexico, after Mexico won its independence from Spain. Mexico then lost the territory to the United States during the Mexican War (1846–1848). The New Mexico Territory was established in 1850. In 1912 New Mexico became the forty-seventh state.

Historic sites and other attractions: Carlsbad Caverns National Park, Puyé Cliff Dwellings, San Miguel Mission, Glorietta Battle Site, Los Alamos Bradbury Science Hall and Museum, White Sands National Monument

Unusual facts: The first atomic bomb was built at Los Alamos Laboratory and exploded near Alamogordo. The oldest highway in the United States is El Camino Real, first used in 1581. One of the world's largest known systems of caves is Carlsbad Caverns. The oldest government building in the United States is the Palace of the Governors, built by Spanish settlers in Santa Fe in 1610.

Original American Indian groups: Apache, Navajo, Pueblo (Keresan, Shoshoni, Zuni)

Harcourt Brace School Publishers

THE MAP BOOK

Name _____

N E
W S

Harcourt Brace School Publishers

60 Miles

90 Kilometers

30   60

30

0   0

FACTS ABOUT
NEW YORK

Population: 18,137,000

Capital: Albany

State nickname: Empire State

Largest cities: New York City, Buffalo, Rochester, Yonkers, Syracuse

Major land areas: Adirondack Mountains, Appalachian Mountains, Appalachian Plateau, Atlantic Coastal Plain, Central Plains, Hudson-Mohawk Lowland, New England Upland

Lowest point: Along the Atlantic Ocean, sea level

Highest point: Mount Marcy, 5,344 feet (1,629 m)

Major rivers: Allegheny River, Delaware River, East River, Genesee River, Hudson River, Mohawk River, Niagara River, Oswego River, St. Lawrence River, Seneca River, Susquehanna River

Major bodies of water: Allegheny Reservoir, Chautauqua Lake, Finger Lakes, Lake Champlain, Lake Erie, Lake George, Lake Oneida, Lake Ontario, Lake Placid, Long Island Sound, Niagara Falls, Saranac Lakes

Climate: In January temperatures range from 11°F (-12°C) to 30°F (-1°C) in the east and from 17°F (-8°C) to 30°F (-1°C) in the west. In July temperatures range from 60°F (16°C) to 84°F (29°C) in the east and from 62°F (17°C) to 80°F (27°C) in the west. The average yearly precipitation is 36 inches (91 cm) in the east and 39 inches (99 cm) in the west.

Resources, industries, and products: Finance, communications, tourism, printing and publishing, pharmaceuticals, machinery, instruments, toys and sporting goods, electronics, apples, grapes, strawberries, milk, cheese

History: Henry Hudson explored the Hudson River in 1609. Dutch settlers established New Amsterdam (New York City) in 1625. The English seized the territory from the Dutch in 1664 and renamed the area New York. In 1788 New York became the eleventh state.

Historic sites and other attractions: Niagara Falls, Fort Ticonderoga, Saratoga National Historical Park, Statue of Liberty National Monument, United Nations, Empire State Building, Metropolitan Museum of Art, Franklin D. Roosevelt National Historic Site

Unusual facts: The first women's suffrage convention in the United States was held in Seneca Falls in 1848. New York City was the capital of the United States from 1785 to 1790. New York City is the largest city in the United States, the second-largest city in the world, and one of the world's biggest and busiest seaports.

Original American Indian groups: Delaware, Erie, Iroquois, Mahican, Mohegan, Montauk, Neutrals, Sapono, Tuscarora, Tutelo, Wappinger

State flower: Rose

State bird: Bluebird

Harcourt Brace School Publishers

THE MAP BOOK

Name _____

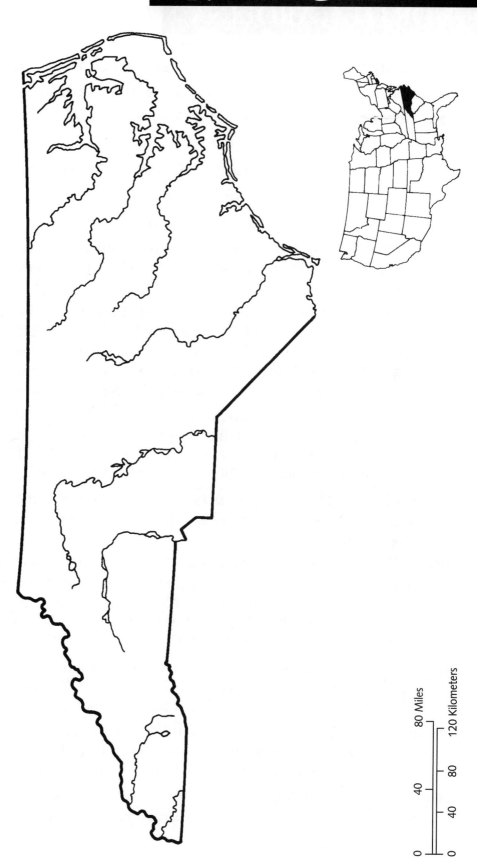

80 Miles

120 Kilometers

40

80

80

40

40

0

0

Harcourt Brace School Publishers

THE MAP BOOK

Name _____

NORTH CAROLINA

Population: 7,425,000

Capital: Raleigh

State flower: Dogwood

State bird: Cardinal

State nicknames: Tar Heel State, Old North State

Largest cities: Charlotte, Raleigh, Greensboro, Winston-Salem, Durham

Major land areas: Atlantic Coastal Plain, Blue Ridge Mountains, Piedmont

Lowest point: Along the Atlantic coast, sea level

Highest point: Mount Mitchell, 6,684 feet (2,037 m)

Major rivers: Cape Fear River, Catawba River, Hiwassee River, Little Tennessee River, Nantahala River, Neuse River, Pee Dee River, Roanoke River, Tar River, Yadkin River

Major bodies of water: Albemarle Sound, Badin Lake (artificial), Blewett Falls Lake (artificial), Fontana Lake, High Rock Lake (artificial), B. Everett Jordan Lake, Lake Gaston, Lake Hickory (artificial), Lake Hiwassee (artificial), Lake James (artificial), Lake Mattamuskeet, Lake Norman (artificial), Lake Phelps, Lake Tillery (artificial), Pamlico Sound, W. Kerr Scott Reservoir

Climate: In January temperatures average 39 °F (4 °C) in the northeast and 36 °F (2 °C) in the western mountains. In July temperatures average 78 °F (26 °C) in the northeast and 73 °F (23 °C) in the western mountains. The average yearly precipitation is 45 inches (114 cm) throughout the state.

Resources, industries, and products: Tobacco, tourism, textiles, rubber and plastic products, electrical and electronic equipment, chemicals, furniture, corn, cotton, peanuts, cattle

History: In 1524 Giovanni da Verrazano landed on the North Carolina coast. In 1585 the English established their first settlement in America at Roanoke Island. In the seventeenth century, North Carolina became an English proprietary colony. In 1776 the colony claimed its independence and wrote a state constitution. In 1789 North Carolina became the twelfth state.

Historic sites and other attractions: Alamance Battlefield, Wright Brothers National Memorial, Cape Hatteras, Tryon Palace, Ocracoke Island, Chimney Rock, Grandfather Mountain, Great Smoky Mountains National Park

Unusual facts: The University of North Carolina was the nation's first state university. The first airplane flight took place at Kitty Hawk in 1903. Colonists settled on Roanoke Island in 1585, but later mysteriously vanished.

Original American Indian groups: Cape Fear, Cheraw, Chowanoc, Coree, Enox Hatteras, Machapunga, Shakori, Tuscarora, Weapemeoc

Harcourt Brace School Publishers

THE MAP BOOK

Name _____

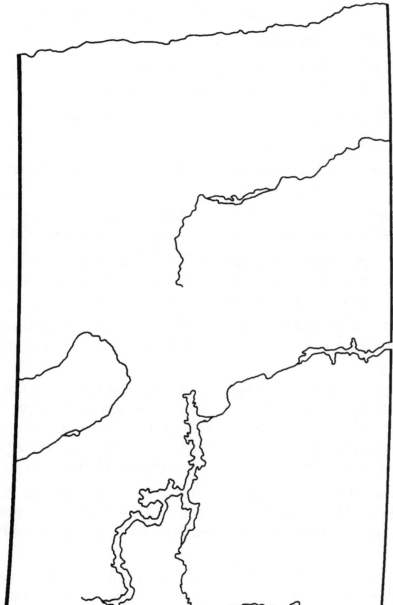

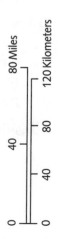

FACTS ABOUT
NORTH DAKOTA

Population: 640,000

Capital: Bismarck

State flower: Wild prairie rose

State bird: Western meadowlark

State nicknames: Flickertail State, Peace Garden State

Largest cities: Fargo, Grand Forks, Bismarck, Minot, Dickinson

Major land areas: Central Plains, Great Plains, Red River Valley

Lowest point: In Pembina County, 750 feet (229 m) above sea level

Highest point: White Butte, 3,506 feet (1,069 m)

Major rivers: James River, Little Missouri River, Missouri River, Red River, Souris River

Major bodies of water: Devils Lake, Jamestown Reservoir, Lake Darling (artificial), Lake Oahe (artificial), Lake Sakakawea (artificial), Long Lake

Climate: In January temperatures range from -2 °F (-19 °C) to 20 °F (-7 °C), and in July temperatures range from 56 °F (13 °C) to 84 °F (29 °C). Throughout the state, the average yearly precipitation is 15 inches (38 cm).

Resources, industries, and products: Telecommunications, energy, farm equipment, food processing, spring wheat, barley, rye, flaxseed, potatoes, sugar beets, cattle, lime

History: In 1682 France claimed the region, but explorers did not arrive there until 1738. In 1762 France gave the region west of the Missouri to Spain. Spain then returned the land to France in 1800. The United States bought the territory as part of the Louisiana Purchase in 1803. By 1812 settlers began moving to the region. In 1889 North Dakota became the thirty-ninth state.

Historic sites and other attractions: Theodore Roosevelt National Park, Writing Rock, Burning Lignite Beds, Knife River Indian Villages National Historic Site, Lake Sakakawea, Fort Abraham Lincoln State Park, International Peace Garden

Unusual facts: The Red River Valley is one of the most fertile regions in the world. North Dakota is usually second to Kansas in wheat production. Garrison Dam is one of the largest dams in the world. North Dakota was named for the Sioux Indians of the territory. The Sioux Indian word *Dakota* means "friends." The geographic center of North America is near Rugby.

Original American Indian groups: Arikara, Cheyenne, Hidatsa, Mandan

Harcourt Brace School Publishers

THE MAP BOOK

OHIO

N
W · E
S

| 0 | 25 | 50 Miles |
| 0 | 25 | 50 | 75 Kilometers |

FACTS ABOUT
OHIO

Population: 11,186,000

Capital: Columbus

State nickname: Buckeye State

State flower: Scarlet carnation

State bird: Cardinal

Largest cities: Columbus, Cleveland, Cincinnati, Toledo, Akron

Major land areas: Appalachian Plateau, Bluegrass Region, Central Plains

Lowest point: Along the Ohio River in Hamilton County, 433 feet (132 m) above sea level

Highest point: Campbell Hill, 1,550 feet (472 m)

Major rivers: Maumee River, Miami River, Muskingum River, Ohio River, Scioto River

Major bodies of water: Dillon Lake, Grand Lake (artificial), Lake Erie, Miami and Erie Canal, Ohio and Erie Canal

Climate: Temperatures average 26°F (-3°C) in January and 73°F (23°C) in July. The average yearly precipitation is 38 inches (97 cm).

Resources, industries, and products: Trade, services, transportation equipment, machinery, corn, hay, winter wheat, oats, soybeans, chickens, turkeys, fishing

History: Ohio was explored by the French in the seventeenth century. In 1763 the British won possession of the territory after defeating the French in the French and Indian War. The United States won control of Ohio after the American Revolution. Ohio was part of the Northwest Territory established in 1787. In 1803 Ohio became the seventeenth state.

Historic sites and other attractions: Adena State Memorial, Great Serpent Mound, National Professional Football Hall of Fame, Schoenbrunn Village, Fort Recovery, United States Air Force Museum, Neil Armstrong Air and Space Museum

Unusual facts: Seven Presidents were born in Ohio: Ulysses S. Grant, Rutherford B. Hayes, James A. Garfield, Benjamin Harrison, William McKinley, Warren G. Harding, and William Howard Taft. The first professional baseball team was the Cincinnati Red Stockings, formed in 1869. Oberlin College, established in 1833, was the first coeducational college in the United States. Ohio is the home of many inventions, including the process of aluminum refining, the cash register, and the automobile self-starter. Ohio is fourth, after California, New York, and Texas, among the leading industrial states.

Original American Indian groups: Erie, Mosopelea, Shawnee, Wyandot (Huron)

Harcourt Brace School Publishers

THE MAP BOOK

Name _____

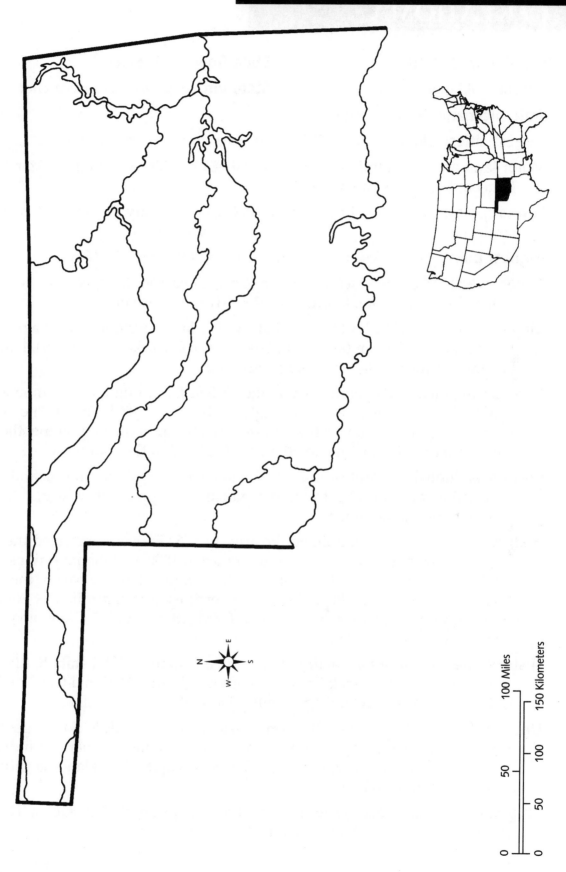

Harcourt Brace School Publishers

100 Miles

150 Kilometers

Name _____

FACTS ABOUT
OKLAHOMA

Population: 3,317,000

Capital: Oklahoma City

State nickname: Sooner State

State flower: Mistletoe

State bird: Scissor-tailed flycatcher

Largest cities: Oklahoma City, Tulsa, Lawton, Norman, Broken Arrow

Major land areas: Central Plains, Great Plains, Ouachita Mountains, Ozark Plateau, Red River Valley Region

Lowest point: Along the Little River in McCurtain County, 287 feet (87 m) above sea level

Highest point: Black Mesa in Cimarron County, 4,973 feet (1,516 m)

Major rivers: Arkansas River, Canadian River, Cimarron River, Neosho River, North Canadian River, North Fork Red River, Red River

Major bodies of water: Fort Gibson Lake (artificial), Keystone Lake, Lake Eufaula, Lake Hudson (artificial), Lake O'The Cherokees (artificial), Lake Texoma (artificial), Robert S. Kerr Reservoir

Climate: In January temperatures average 39°F (4°C) throughout Oklahoma. In July the average temperature throughout the state is 83°F (28°C). The average yearly precipitation ranges from 15 inches (38 cm) in the Panhandle, the western part of Oklahoma, to 50 inches (127 cm) in the southeast.

Resources, industries, and products: Mineral and energy exploration and production, machinery, petroleum products, food products, wheat, cotton, peanuts, coal, cattle, stone

History: In 1682 the French claimed the area. In 1762 France transferred the region to Spain, which returned it to France in 1800. Oklahoma (minus its Panhandle) was then sold by France to the United States as part of the Louisiana Purchase of 1803. The eastern territory was controlled by American Indian groups until after the Civil War (1861–1865). In 1907 Oklahoma became the forty-sixth state.

Historic sites and other attractions: Will Rogers Memorial, Washita Battlefield, Woolaroc Museum, Creek Capitol, Dinosaur Quarry, National Cowboy Hall of Fame and Western Heritage Center, Tsa-La-Gi Ancient Village

Unusual facts: In 1889, when Oklahoma was opened to settlers, 50,000 people moved there in a single day. Oklahoma is home to more American Indians than any other state except Arizona. The state capitol in Oklahoma City stands on a major oil field.

Original American Indian groups: Arapaho, Comanche, Kichai, Kiowa, Kiowa Apache, Okmulgee, Osage, Wichita

Harcourt Brace School Publishers

Name _____

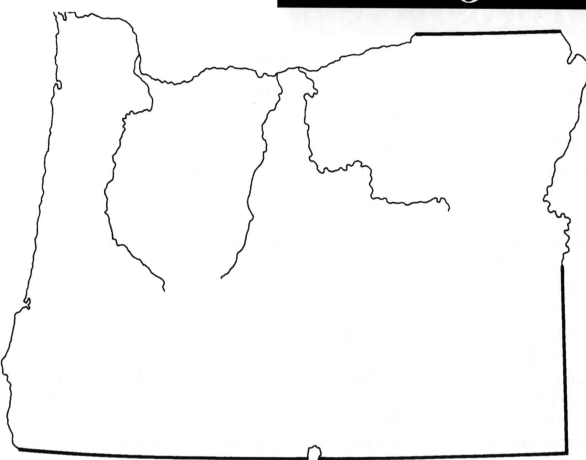

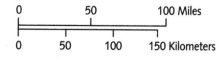

N
W E
S

0   50   100 Miles

0   50   100   150 Kilometers

Harcourt Brace School Publishers

Name _____

OREGON

Population: 3,243,000

Capital: Salem

State nickname: Beaver State

State flower: Oregon grape

State bird: Western meadowlark

Largest cities: Portland, Eugene, Salem, Gresham, Beaverton

Major land areas: Basin and Range Region, Cascade Range, Coast Ranges, Columbia Plateau

Lowest point: Along the Pacific Ocean, sea level

Highest point: Mount Hood in Clackamas and Hood River counties, 11,235 feet (3,424 m)

Major rivers: Columbia River, Deschutes River, John Day River, Snake River, Willamette River

Major bodies of water: Crater Lake, Harney Lake, Lake Owyhee, Malheur Lake, Upper Klamath Lake, Wallowa Lake

Climate: In January temperatures range from 34°F (1°C) to 45°F (7°C), and in July temperatures range from 57°F (14°C) to 80°F (27°C). The average yearly precipitation is 36 inches (91 cm).

Resources, industries, and products: Forestry, tourism, high technology, lumber and wood products, foods, paper, metals, wheat, fishing, cattle

History: Explorers may have reached Oregon in the sixteenth century. The first settlement, a fur-trading post, was established in 1811 by John Jacob Astor at Astoria. In 1843 large migrations of settlers began. In 1848 Oregon became a territory, and it became the thirty-third state in 1859.

Historic sites and other attractions: Columbia River Gorge, Fort Clatsop National Memorial, Crater Lake National Park, Mount Hood National Forest, Picture Gorge, Sea Lion Caves, Shakespeare Festival

Unusual facts: Oregon leads the nation in timber production. The name *Oregon* comes from the French word meaning "hurricane," which was used to describe the mighty Columbia River. The Columbia River was named after the ship of an early explorer, Captain Robert Gray, who sailed into the river in 1792. Crater Lake is the deepest lake in the United States. Its depth is 1,932 feet (589 m), and it lies in the crater of an extinct volcano.

Original American Indian groups: Calapooya, Chastacosta, Chinook, Clackamas, Klamath, Modoc, Siuslaw, Takelma, Tillamook, Tuturui

THE MAP BOOK

Name _____

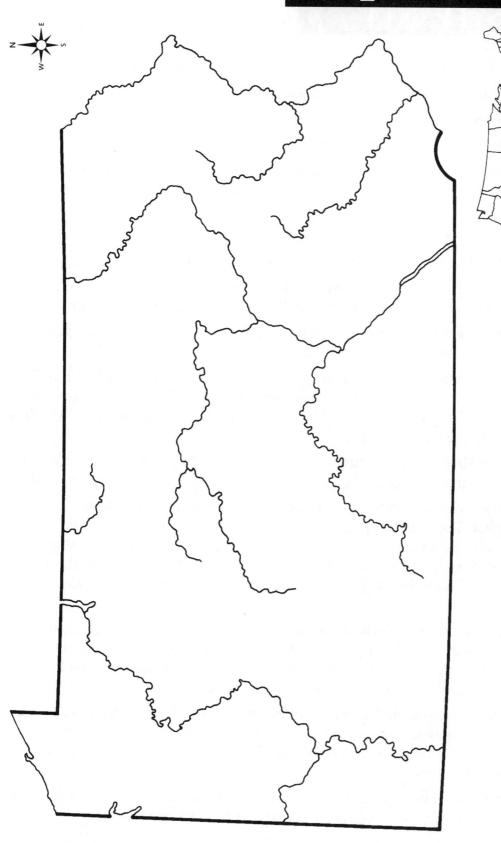

Harcourt Brace School Publishers

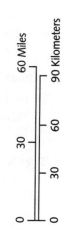

Name _____

PENNSYLVANIA

Population: 12,019,000

Capital: Harrisburg

State nickname: Keystone State

State flower: Mountain laurel

State bird: Ruffed grouse

Largest cities: Philadelphia, Pittsburgh, Erie, Allentown, Scranton

Major land areas: Appalachian Mountains, Appalachian Plateau, Atlantic Coastal Plain, Blue Ridge Mountains, Central Plains, New England Upland, Piedmont

Lowest point: Along the Delaware River, sea level

Highest point: Mount Davis in Somerset County, 3,213 feet (979 m)

Major rivers: Allegheny River, Delaware River, Juniata River, Lehigh River, Monongahela River, Ohio River, Schuylkill River, Susquehanna River

Major bodies of water: Allegheny Reservoir, Lake Erie, Lake Wallenpaupack, Pymatuning Reservoir, Raystown Lake (artificial)

Climate: In January temperatures average 27°F (-3°C) in the north and 31°F (-1°C) in the southeast. In July temperatures average 73°F (23°C) in the northwest and 77°F (25°C) in the southeast. The average yearly precipitation is 39 inches (99 cm) throughout the state.

Resources, industries, and products: Steel, travel, health, electrical and nonelectrical machinery, metals, foods, glass products, corn, hay, mushrooms, coal

History: In 1643 Swedish settlers established a colony on Tinicum Island, near Philadelphia. The Dutch captured the region from the Swedes in 1655, and the English took control of the area in 1664. In 1681 Pennsylvania was given to William Penn. The Declaration of Independence was adopted by the 13 colonies in Philadelphia in 1776. In 1787 Pennsylvania became the second state.

Historic sites and other attractions: Independence National Historical Park, Gettysburg National Military Park, Valley Forge, Pine Creek Gorge, Hawk Mountain Bird Sanctuary, Franklin Institute Science Museum, Pennsylvania Farm Museum of Landis Valley, Mummers' Parade on New Year's Day

Unusual facts: Pennsylvania leads the nation in steel production. KDKA, started in 1920, was one of the first radio stations in the country. The Pennsylvania Turnpike was the nation's first paved road. The world's largest chocolate factory is in Hershey.

Original American Indian groups: Delaware, Erie, Honniasont, Iroquois, Saluda, Saponi, Shawnee, Susquehanna, Tuscarora, Tutelo, Wenrohronon

Harcourt Brace School Publishers

THE MAP BOOK

Name _____

Harcourt Brace School Publishers

0   5   10 Miles

0   5   10   15 Kilometers

FACTS ABOUT
RHODE ISLAND

Population: 987,000

Capital: Providence

State flower: Violet

State bird: Rhode Island red (chicken)

State nicknames: Ocean State, Little Rhody

Largest cities: Providence, Warwick, Cranston, Pawtucket, East Providence

Major land areas: Coastal Lowlands, New England Upland

Lowest point: Along the Atlantic coast, sea level

Highest point: Jerimoth Hill, 812 feet (247 m)

Major rivers: Blackstone River, Pawcatuck River, Providence River, Sakonnet River, Seekonk River, Woonasquatucket River

Major bodies of water: Narragansett Bay, Rhode Island Sound, Scituate Reservoir, Watchaug Pond, Worden Pond

Climate: In January temperatures average 28°F (-2°C) throughout the state, and in July temperatures average 73°F (23°C). The average yearly precipitation is 46 inches (117 cm).

Resources, industries, and products: Costume jewelry, toys, machinery, textiles, electronics, turf, potatoes, apples, fishing, sand and gravel

History: In 1524 Giovanni da Verrazano sailed into Narragansett Bay. The Dutch navigator Adriaen Block also explored the region in 1614. Providence was founded in 1636 by Roger Williams. In 1644 Williams got a charter from England for the colony of Rhode Island. In 1790 Rhode Island became the thirteenth state.

Historic sites and other attractions: Gilbert Stuart's Birthplace, Old Stone Mill, General Nathanael Greene Homestead, Slater Mill Historic Site, Newport, Block Island and Souteast Lighthouse

Unusual facts: Rhode Island is the smallest state and is therefore often called Little Rhody. It has the longest official name of any state: State of Rhode Island and Providence Plantations. Rhode Island was the first of the original 13 colonies to declare independence from Britain. Touro Synagogue, built in 1763, is the oldest synagogue in the United States still in use today. Providence is the leading center of jewelry manufacturing in the nation. The Slater Mill, built in 1793 in Pawtucket, was one of North America's first textile mills.

Original American Indian groups: Narragansett, Niantic (Eastern), Nipmuck, Pequot, Wampanoag

Harcourt Brace School Publishers

Name _____

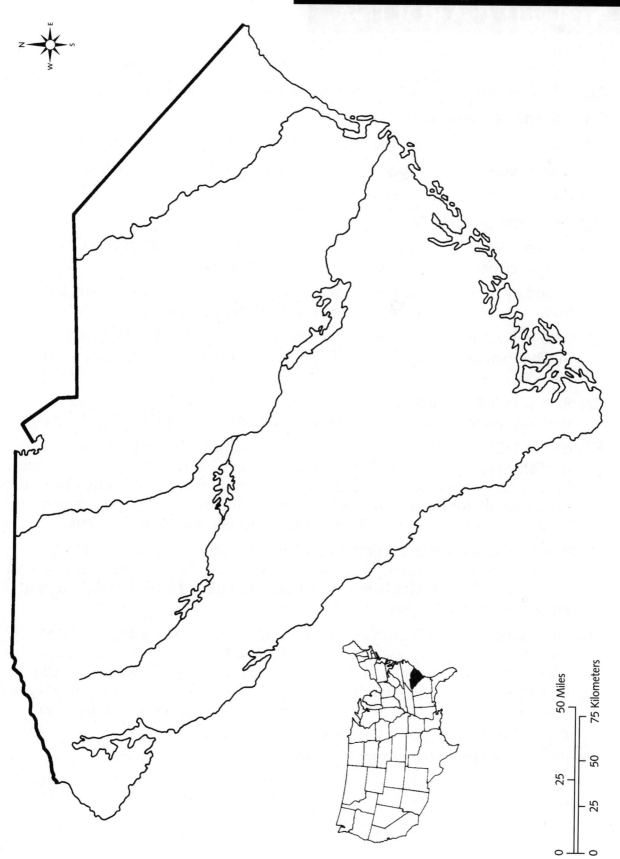

N
E
W
S

Harcourt Brace School Publishers

50 Miles

0   25   50   75 Kilometers

0   25   50

FACTS ABOUT
SOUTH CAROLINA

Population: 3,760,000

Capital: Columbia

State nickname: Palmetto State

State flower: Yellow jessamine

State bird: Carolina wren

Largest cities: Columbia, Charleston, North Charleston, Greenville, Spartanburg

Major land areas: Atlantic Coastal Plain, Blue Ridge Mountains, Piedmont

Lowest point: Along the Atlantic Ocean, sea level

Highest point: Sassafras Mountain, 3,560 feet (1,085 m)

Major rivers: Broad River, Chattooga River, Congaree River, Edisto River, Pee Dee River, Saluda River, Santee River, Savannah River

Major bodies of water: Clark Hill Lake, Hartwell Lake, Lake Greenwood, Lake Marion, Lake Moultrie, Lake Murray, Lake Wateree, Lake Wylie (all artificial)

Climate: In January temperatures range from 38°F (3°C) to 58°F (14°C), and in July temperatures range from 73°F (23°C) to 90°F (32°C). The average yearly precipitation is 52 inches (132 cm).

Resources, industries, and products: Tourism, textiles, chemicals, machinery, clothing, soybeans, corn, cotton, peaches, tobacco, chickens, fishing, petroleum

History: In 1521 Spanish explorers reached the coastline of South Carolina. The English established the first permanent settlement in 1670 on Albemarle Point. In 1680 that colony moved to Charleston. In time, the name of South Carolina came into use for the southern part of the colony. The northern settlements became North Carolina. In 1788 South Carolina became the eighth state.

Historic sites and other attractions: Fort Sumter National Monument, Kings Mountain National Military Park, Cypress Gardens, Fort Moultrie, Cowpens National Battlefield, Middleton Place Gardens, Hilton Head Island, Windmill Point, Myrtle Beach, Charleston Museum

Unusual facts: It was in South Carolina, around 1685, that rice was first raised successfully in North America. One of the oldest museums in the country is the Charleston Museum, founded in 1773. South Carolina was the first state to withdraw from the Union before the Civil War. The Civil War began at Fort Sumter on April 12, 1861. South Carolina is a leader among the states in the production of textiles and peaches.

Original American Indian groups: Catawba, Cusabo

Harcourt Brace School Publishers

Name _____

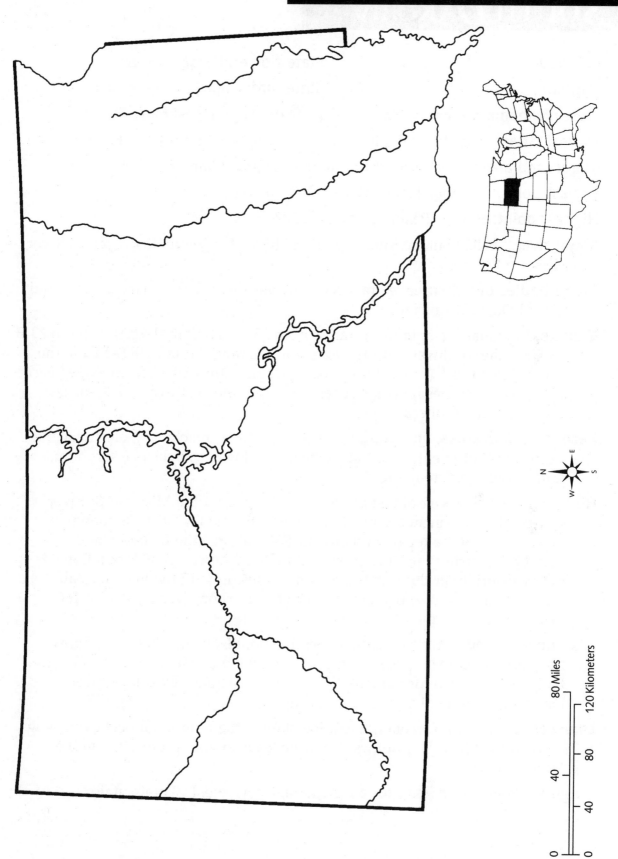

Harcourt Brace School Publishers

80 Miles

120 Kilometers

40

80

40

0

0

Name _____

FACTS ABOUT
SOUTH DAKOTA

Population: 737,000

Capital: Pierre

State flower: Pasqueflower

State bird: Chinese ring-necked pheasant

State nicknames: Sunshine State, Coyote State, Mount Rushmore State

Largest cities: Sioux Falls, Rapid City, Aberdeen, Watertown, Brookings

Major land areas: Black Hills, Central Plains, Great Plains

Lowest point: Big Stone Lake, 962 feet (293 m) above sea level

Highest point: Harney Peak, 7,242 feet (2,207 m)

Major rivers: Belle Fourche River, Big Sioux River, Cheyenne River, James River, Missouri River

Major bodies of water: Lake Francis Case, Lake Oahe, Lake Sharpe, Lewis and Clark Lake (all artificial)

Climate: In January temperatures range from 13°F (-11°C) in the northeast to 23°F (-5°C) in the southwest. In July temperatures range from 72°F (22°C) in the Black Hills to 75°F (24°C) throughout the rest of the state. The average yearly precipitation ranges from 17 inches (43 cm) in the northwest to 20 inches (51 cm) in the southeast.

Resources, industries, and products: Food products, machinery, electrical and electronic equipment, corn, oats, wheat, sunflowers, soybeans, sorghum, cattle, hogs, gold, tourism

History: In 1682 France claimed all the land drained by the Mississippi River system. This area included present-day South Dakota. The first known explorations of the region occurred in 1743. In 1803 the United States bought the territory in the Louisiana Purchase. Lewis and Clark followed the Missouri River through the region in 1804. In 1817 the French established the first permanent settlement. The Dakota Territory was created in 1861. In 1889 South Dakota became the fortieth state.

Historic sites and other attractions: Deadwood, Black Hills National Forest, Mount Rushmore National Memorial, Crazy Horse Memorial, Corn Palace, Badlands National Monument, "Great Lakes of South Dakota," Jewel Cave National Monument

Unusual facts: South Dakota is a leading state in the number of beef cattle, hogs, and lambs raised. The Homestake Mine leads in gold production in the United States.

Original American Indian groups: Arikara, Cheyenne, Dakota, Sutaio

Harcourt Brace School Publishers

THE MAP BOOK

Name _____

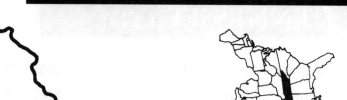

_T_ENNESSEE

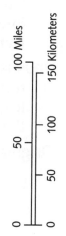

FACTS ABOUT
*T*ENNESSEE

Population: 5,368,000

Capital: Nashville

State nickname: Volunteer State

State flower: Iris

State bird: Mockingbird

Largest cities: Memphis, Nashville, Knoxville, Chattanooga, Clarksville

Major land areas: Appalachian Mountains, Appalachian Plateau, Blue Ridge Mountains, Gulf Coastal Plain, Interior Low Plateau, Mississippi Alluvial Plain

Lowest point: Along the Mississippi River in Shelby County, 182 feet (55 m) above sea level

Highest point: Clingmans Dome, 6,643 feet (2,025 m)

Major rivers: Cumberland River, Mississippi River, Tennessee River

Major bodies of water: Dale Hollow Lake, Kentucky Lake, Lake Barkley, Lake Chickamauga, Pickwick Lake, Watts Bar Lake (all artificial)

Climate: In January temperatures range from 37°F (3°C) in the north to 40°F (4°C) in the south. In July temperatures range from 80°F (27°C) in the north to 83°F (28°C) in the south. Most of the state averages 50 inches (127 cm) of precipitation a year.

Resources, industries, and products: Trade, tourism, finance, real estate, chemicals, transportation equipment, food, machinery, rubber products, tobacco, cotton, lint, soybeans, cattle, hogs, coal

History: In 1540 Hernando de Soto explored the Tennessee region for Spain. In 1682 France claimed the Mississippi River valley. France later lost the area to the British in 1763, after the French and Indian War. In 1796 Tennessee became the sixteenth state.

Historic sites and other attractions: Andrew Johnson National Historic Site, Great Smoky Mountains National Park, American Museum of Science and Energy, Grand Ole Opry House, Shiloh National Military Park, The Hermitage, Lookout Mountain, Graceland (the home of Elvis Presley)

Unusual facts: The Watauga Association drew up one of the first written constitutions in North America, in 1772. Tennessee was the last Confederate state to leave the Union and the first to be readmitted. The Parthenon in Nashville is the world's only reproduction of the ancient Greek temple.

Original American Indian groups: Cherokee, Chickasaw, Kaskinampo, Shawnee

Harcourt Brace School Publishers

THE MAP BOOK

Name _____

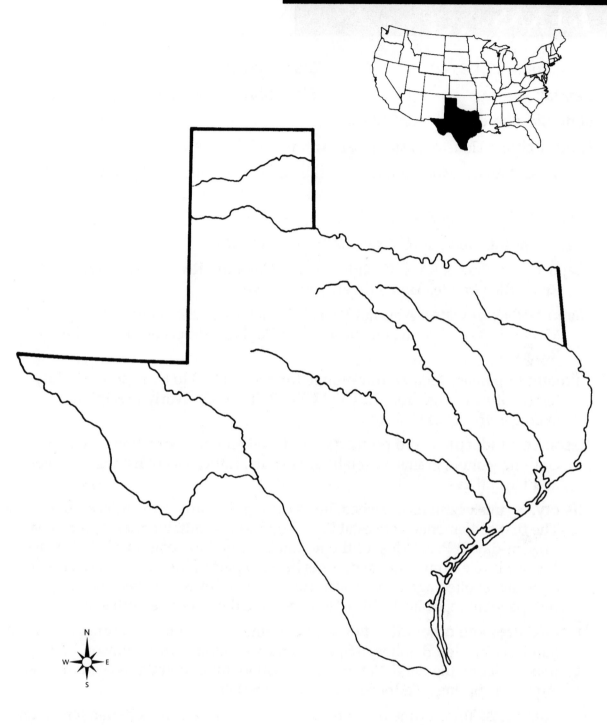

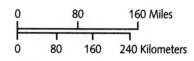

0   80   160 Miles

0   80   160   240 Kilometers

Harcourt Brace School Publishers

THE MAP BOOK

FACTS ABOUT
*T*EXAS

Population: 19,439,000

Capital: Austin

State nickname: Lone Star State

State flower: Bluebonnet

State bird: Mockingbird

Largest cities: Houston, Dallas, San Antonio, El Paso, Austin

Major land areas: Mountains and Basins, Central Plains, Great Plains, Coastal Plain

Lowest point: Along the Gulf of Mexico, sea level

Highest point: Guadalupe Peak, 8,749 feet (2,667 m)

Major rivers: Brazos River, Canadian River, Colorado River, Pecos River, Red River, Rio Grande, Sabine River, Trinity River

Major bodies of water: Amistad Reservoir, Galveston Bay, Gulf of Mexico, Lake Meredith, Lake Texoma (artificial), Sam Rayburn Reservoir, Toledo Bend Reservoir

Climate: In January temperatures range from 40°F (4°C) to 61°F (16°C). In July temperatures range from 72°F (22°C) to 93°F (34°C). Yearly precipitation averages 46 inches (117 cm).

Resources, industries, and products: Trade, oil and gas extraction, machinery, clothing, cotton, grains, vegetables, peanuts, cattle, sheep, fishing, petroleum and natural gas

History: Spanish explorers reached Texas during the early sixteenth century. The first settlements were established by Spanish missionaries in 1682 near present-day El Paso. Most of the region belonged to Spain until 1821, when Mexico broke from Spain and Texas became part of Mexico. American settlers in Texas revolted against Mexican rule in 1836. Texas then became an independent republic. In 1845 Texas became the twenty-eighth state.

Historic sites and other attractions: The Alamo, San Jacinto Monument, Mission San Jose, Lyndon B. Johnson Space Center, Lyndon Baines Johnson Library and Museum, Big Bend National Park, Guadalupe Mountains National Park, Aquarena Springs, Padre Island National Seashore

Unusual facts: Texas is one of the three states that have been independent countries. (The other two are Hawaii and Vermont.) King Ranch, a cattle ranch in Texas, is about the same size as the state of Rhode Island.

Original American Indian groups: Caddo, Coahuiltecan, Comanche, Karankawa, Lipan, Shuman, Tonkawa, Wichita

Harcourt Brace School Publishers

Name _____

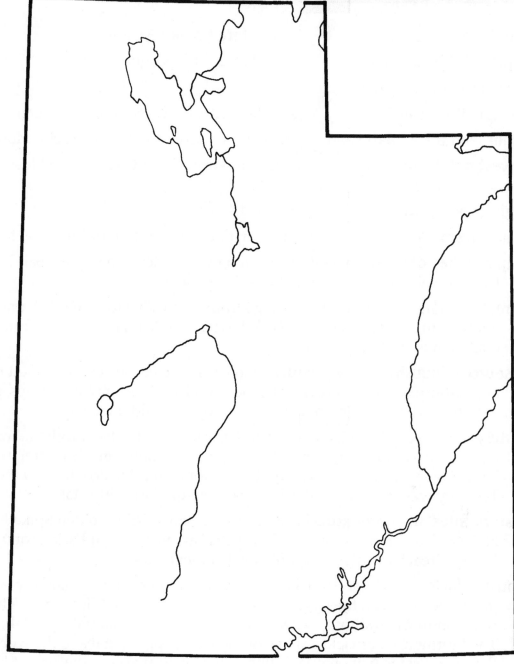

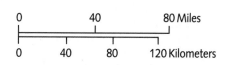

0   40   80 Miles

0   40   80   120 Kilometers

THE MAP BOOK

FACTS ABOUT
U TAH

Population: 2,059,000

Capital: Salt Lake City

State nickname: Beehive State

State flower: Sego lily

State bird: Seagull

Largest cities: Salt Lake City, West Valley City, Provo, Sandy, Orem, Ogden

Major land areas: Basin and Range Region, Colorado Plateau, Rocky Mountains

Lowest point: Along Beaverdam Creek in Washington County, 2,000 feet (610 m) above sea level

Highest point: Kings Peak, 13,528 feet (4,123 m)

Major rivers: Bear River, Colorado River, Green River, Jordan River, Sevier River

Major bodies of water: Bear Lake, Flaming Gorge Reservoir, Great Salt Lake, Lake Powell (artificial), Sevier Lake, Utah Lake

Climate: In January temperatures range from 19°F (-7°C) to 36°F (2°C), and in July temperatures range from 64°F (18°C) to 92°F (33°C). The average yearly precipitation is 16 inches (41 cm).

Resources, industries, and products: Government, construction, guided missiles and parts, electronic components, food products, automobile airbags, steel, coal, hay, wheat, apples, onions, pears, copper, gold, metals

History: Two Spanish explorers came to Utah in 1776. In 1847 Brigham Young led a group of Mormons into the Great Salt Lake region. One year later, the United States won possession of the territory from Mexico. In 1850 the Utah Territory was created. In 1896 Utah became the forty-fifth state.

Historic sites and other attractions: Mormon Tabernacle, Golden Spike National Historic Site, Zion National Park, Bryce Canyon National Park, Monument Valley, Great Salt Lake, Canyonlands National Park

Unusual facts: The Great Salt Lake is up to seven times saltier than any ocean in the world. It is also the largest natural lake west of the Mississippi. The first transcontinental railroad system was completed in Promontory, Utah, in 1869. The Mormon Tabernacle has one of the largest pipe organs in the world. Rainbow Bridge National Monument, in Glen Canyon, is the largest known natural stone bridge in the world.

Original American Indian groups: Gosiute, Southern Paiute, Ute, Western Shoshoni

Harcourt Brace School Publishers

Name _____

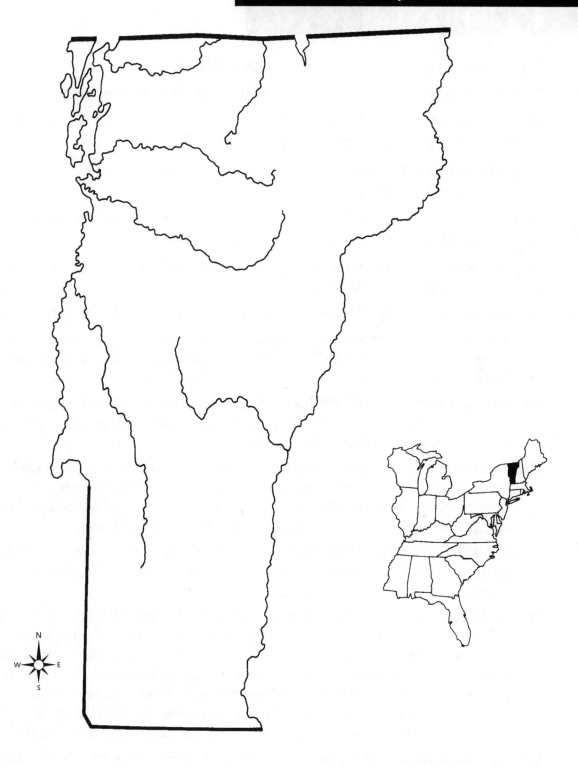

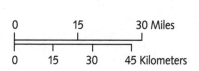

0   15   30 Miles

0   15   30   45 Kilometers

Harcourt Brace School Publishers

THE MAP BOOK

FACTS ABOUT
VERMONT

Population: 588,000

Capital: Montpelier

State flower: Red clover

State bird: Hermit thrush

State nickname: Green Mountain State

Largest cities: Burlington, Rutland, Bennington, Barre, Hartford

Major land areas: Appalachian Mountains, Green Mountains, New England Upland, White Mountains

Lowest point: Lake Champlain in Franklin County, 95 feet (29 m) above sea level

Highest point: Mount Mansfield, 4,393 feet (1,339 m)

Major rivers: Connecticut River, Lamoille River, Missisquoi River, Otter Creek (river), White River, Winooski River

Major bodies of water: Bomoseen Lake, Lake Champlain, Lake Memphremagog

Climate: In January temperatures average 17°F (-8°C) throughout the state. In July temperatures average 71°F (22°C). The average yearly precipitation is 34 inches (86 cm).

Resources, industries, and products: Tourism, finance, real estate, machine tools, furniture, scales, books, computer equipment, fishing rods, dairy products, apples, maple syrup, asbestos, granite

History: In 1609 the Vermont region was claimed by the French. Massachusetts established the first permanent settlement there in 1724. Britain gained control of the region in 1763, but Vermont settlers created an independent republic in 1777. In 1791 Vermont became the fourteenth state.

Historic sites and other attractions: Bennington Battle Monument, Coolidge Birthplace, Old Constitution House, Green Mountain National Forest, Smuggler's Notch, Shelburne Museum

Unusual facts: Vermont is one of the three states that have been independent countries. (The other two are Hawaii and Texas.) Vermont was the first state after the original 13 colonies to enter the Union. Many of the smaller communities in Vermont have a town meeting form of government in which the people take a direct part. Vermont is the only New England state that does not have an Atlantic coastline. Lake Champlain is the largest lake in New England. The largest granite quarries in the United States are near Barre.

Original American Indian groups: Abenaki, Mahican, Pennacook, Pocomtuc

Harcourt Brace School Publishers

VIRGINIA

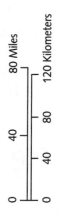

FACTS ABOUT
VIRGINIA

Population: 6,733,000

Capital: Richmond

State nickname: Old Dominion

State flower: Dogwood

State bird: Cardinal

Largest cities: Virginia Beach, Norfolk, Richmond, Newport News, Arlington

Major land areas: Appalachian Mountains, Appalachian Plateau, Atlantic Coastal Plain, Blue Ridge Mountains, Piedmont

Lowest point: Along the Atlantic coast, sea level

Highest point: Mount Rogers, 5,729 feet (1,746 m)

Major rivers: James River, New River, Potomac River, Rappahannock River, Roanoke River, Shenandoah River, York River

Major bodies of water: Chesapeake Bay, Kerr Reservoir, Lake Anna, Lake Drummond, Smith Mountain Lake (artificial)

Climate: In January temperatures average 39°F (4°C) in the coastal region and 36°F (2°C) in parts of the Blue Ridge Mountains. In July temperatures average 78°F (26°C) throughout the state. The average yearly precipitation is 43 inches (109 cm) in the Shenandoah Valley and 45 inches (114 cm) in the southern part of the state.

Resources, industries, and products: Tourism, textiles, transportation equipment, electrical and electronic equipment, food processing, chemicals, printing, soybeans, tobacco, peanuts, corn, apples, cattle, chickens, turkeys, fishing, coal, shipbuilding

History: The first settlers in Virginia, who were Spanish, came in 1570. The first permanent settlement was established by the English in Jamestown in 1607. The Virginia Colony declared its independence from Britain in 1776. In 1788 Virginia became the tenth state.

Historic sites and other attractions: Skyline Drive, Virginia Beach, Arlington National Cemetery, Mount Vernon, Monticello, Williamsburg, Manassas National Battlefield Park, Appomattox Court House

Unusual facts: The College of William and Mary, founded in 1693, is the second-oldest college in the United States. The world's largest shipyard is in Newport News. Eight Presidents were born in Virginia: William Henry Harrison, Thomas Jefferson, James Madison, James Monroe, Zachary Taylor, John Tyler, George Washington, and Woodrow Wilson. More Civil War battles were fought in Virginia than in any other state.

Original American Indian groups: Cherokee, Manahoac, Meherrin, Monacan, Nahyssan, Nottoway, Occaneechi, Powhatan, Saponi, Shakori, Shawnee, Tutelo

Harcourt Brace School Publishers

THE MAP BOOK

Name _____

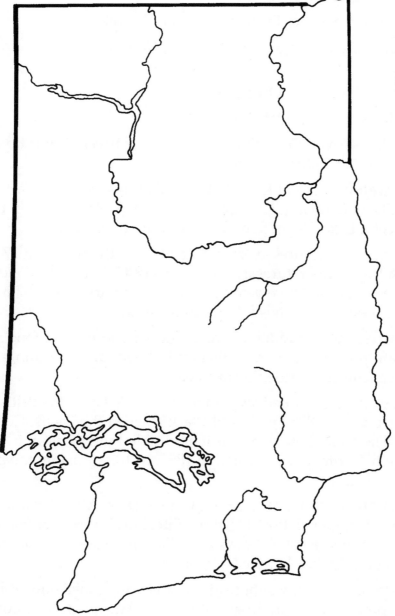

80 Miles

40

40

0

120 Kilometers

80

40

0

Harcourt Brace School Publishers

THE MAP BOOK

Name _____

FACTS ABOUT
WASHINGTON

Population: 5,610,000

Capital: Olympia

State nickname: Evergreen State

State flower: Western rhododendron

State bird: Willow goldfinch

Largest cities: Seattle, Spokane, Tacoma, Bellevue, Everett

Major land areas: Cascade Range, Coast Ranges, Columbia Plateau, Rocky Mountains

Lowest point: Along the Pacific Ocean, sea level

Highest point: Mount Rainier, 14,410 feet (4,392 m)

Major rivers: Chehalis River, Columbia River, Cowlitz River, Skagit River, Snake River, Spokane River, Yakima River

Major bodies of water: Crescent Lake, Franklin D. Roosevelt Lake (artificial), Lake Chelan, Lake Quinault, Lake Sammamish, Lake Washington, Lake Whatcom, Ozette Lake, Puget Sound, Strait of Juan de Fuca

Climate: In January temperatures average 40°F (4°C) in the west and 27°F (-3°C) in the east. In July temperatures average 65°F (18°C) in the west and 69°F (21°C) in the east. The average yearly precipitation varies from 37 inches (94 cm) in the west to 16 inches (41 cm) in the east.

Resources, industries, and products: Forest products, aerospace, food products, metals, aircraft, pulp and paper, lumber and plywood, aluminum, apples, potatoes, sweet cherries, cattle, fishing, coal

History: Spanish explorers claimed Washington in 1775. Later, the British also claimed the region. In 1805 Lewis and Clark reached the Pacific Coast of Washington. The United States and Britain divided the territory in 1846, and the Washington Territory was created in 1853. In 1889 Washington became the forty-second state.

Historic sites and other attractions: Grand Coulee Dam, Mount Rainier National Park, Whitman Mission National Historic Site, Fort Vancouver National Historic Site, San Juan Islands, Lewis and Clark Interpretive Center, North Cascades National Park, Olympic National Park

Unusual facts: Washington grows more apples than any other state. It leads the nation in the production of hydroelectric power. Washington had the most snow recorded in North America for one winter. Mount St. Helens erupted on May 18, 1980.

Original American Indian groups: Chinook, Columbia, Colville, Kalispel, Klickitat, Nisqually, Okanogon, Sanpoil, Spokane, Wallawalla, Wishram, Yakima

Harcourt Brace School Publishers

THE MAP BOOK

Name _____

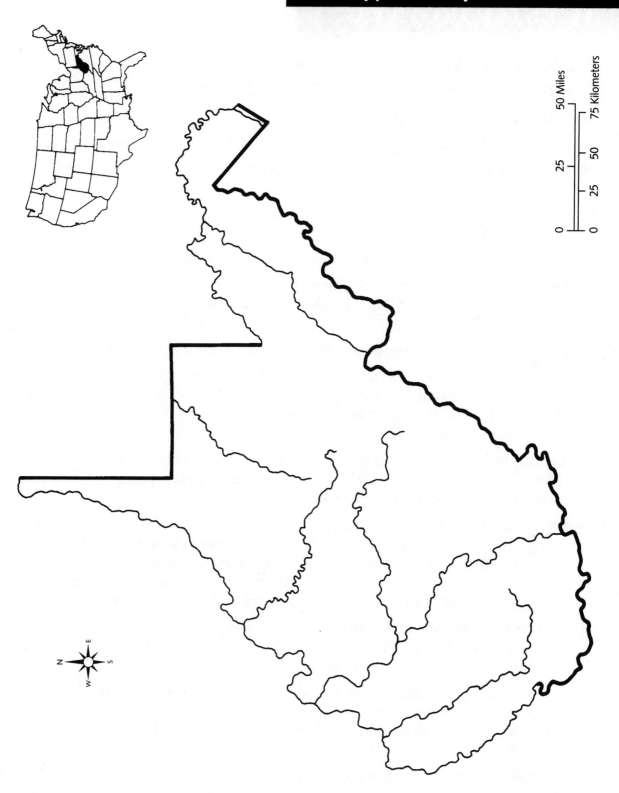

50 Miles

75 Kilometers

Harcourt Brace School Publishers

Name _____

FACTS ABOUT
WEST VIRGINIA

Population: 1,815,000

Capital: Charleston

State nickname: Mountain State

State flower: Big rhododendron

State bird: Cardinal

Largest cities: Charleston, Huntington, Wheeling, Parkersburg, Morgantown

Major land areas: Appalachian Mountains, Appalachian Plateau, Blue Ridge Mountains

Lowest point: Along the Potomac River in Jefferson County, 240 feet (73 m) above sea level

Highest point: Spruce Knob in Pendleton County, 4,861 feet (1,482 m)

Major rivers: Big Sandy River, Elk River, Guyandotte River, Kanawha River, Little Kanawha River, Monongahela River, New River, Ohio River, Potomac River, Shenandoah River

Major bodies of water: Bluestone Lake, E. Lynne Lake, Tygart Lake

Climate: In January temperatures average 33°F (1°C) throughout West Virginia, and in July temperatures average 73°F (23°C). The average yearly precipitation is 60 inches (152 cm) in the mountain regions and 35 inches (89 cm) in the northwest Panhandle.

Resources, industries, and products: Mining, tourism, machinery, plastic and hardwood products, chemicals, aluminum, steel, apples, peaches, tobacco, corn, dairy products, eggs, chickens, coal

History: The West Virginia area was part of the Virginia Colony established by the English in 1606. The first European settlers were Germans seeking religious freedom. Later, the Scotch-Irish established settlements. When Virginia seceded from the Union, the western counties of the region formed a separate state government. In 1863 West Virginia became the thirty-fifth state.

Historic sites and other attractions: Monongahela National Forest, Harpers Ferry National Historical Park, Charles Town, Jackson's Mill, Berkeley Springs, Blennerhassett Island, Seneca Rock

Unusual facts: Ice Mountain, near Racine, has ice at its base throughout the year. Cold air in its underground passages forms the ice and keeps it frozen. The first natural-gas well in the United States was discovered in West Virginia in 1815.

Original American Indian groups: Cherokee, Conoy, Delaware, Honniasont, Moneton, Shawnee, Susquehanna

Harcourt Brace School Publishers

THE MAP BOOK

Name _____

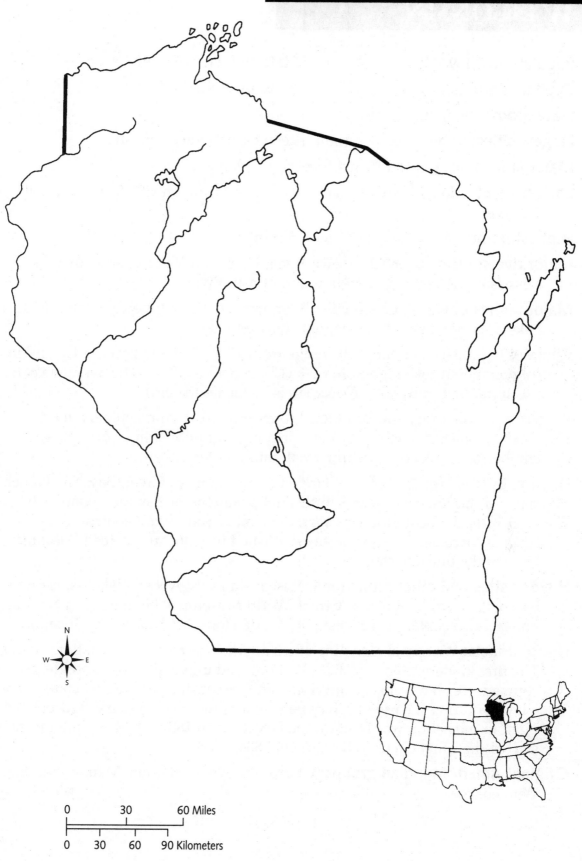

Harcourt Brace School Publishers

N
W E
S

0   30   60 Miles

0   30   60   90 Kilometers

FACTS ABOUT
WISCONSIN

Population: 5,169,000

Capital: Madison

State nickname: Badger State

Largest cities: Milwaukee, Madison, Green Bay, Racine, Kenosha

Major land areas: Central Plains, Superior Upland

Lowest point: Along the western shore of Lake Michigan, 581 feet (177 m) above sea level

Highest point: Timms Hill, 1,951 feet (595 m)

Major rivers: Black River, Chippewa River, Flambeau River, Menominee River, Mississippi River, St. Croix River, Wisconsin River

Major bodies of water: Green Bay, Green Lake, Lake Chippewa, Lake Michigan, Lake Superior, Lake Winnebago, Petenwell Lake

Climate: In January temperatures range from 12°F (-11°C) to 26°F (-3°C), and in July temperatures range from 62°F (17°C) to 80°F (27°C). The average yearly precipitation throughout Wisconsin is 33 inches (84 cm).

Resources, industries, and products: Tourism, industrial machinery, food products, metals, paper products, printing and publishing, corn, peas, cranberries, milk cows, fishing, coal, milk, butter, cheese

History: In 1634 French explorers landed on the shore of Green Bay. The French claimed this area and held it until 1763, when the British took control. In 1783, after the Revolutionary War, the United States won control of the region. Wisconsin Territory was established in 1836, and in 1848 Wisconsin became the thirtieth state.

Historic sites and other attractions: Wisconsin Dells, Apostle Islands, Ice Age National Scientific Reserve, Circus World Museum, Chequamegon National Forest, Nicolet National Forest, Old Wade House and Carriage Museum

Unusual facts: Wisconsin alone produces about 40 percent of the nation's cheese. The first kindergarten, vocational school, and university correspondence course were all developed in Wisconsin. Wisconsin was the first state to pass a law requiring the use of safety belts in automobiles. The first hydroelectric plant in the nation was built on the Fox River in 1882. The Ringling brothers started their first circus at Baraboo in 1884.

Original American Indian groups: Chippewa, Fox, Kickapoo, Menominee, Sauk, Winnebago

State flower: Wood violet

State bird: Robin

Harcourt Brace School Publishers

THE MAP BOOK

WYOMING

Harcourt Brace School Publishers

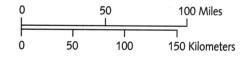

0   50   100 Miles

0   50   100   150 Kilometers

FACTS ABOUT
WYOMING

Population: 479,000

Capital: Cheyenne

State nickname: Equality State

State flower: Indian paintbrush

State bird: Meadowlark

Largest cities: Cheyenne, Casper, Laramie, Rock Springs, Gillette

Major land areas: Great Plains, Rocky Mountains, Wyoming Basin

Lowest point: Belle Fourche River in Crook County, 3,100 feet (945 m) above sea level

Highest point: Gannett Peak in Fremont County, 13,804 feet (4,207 m)

Major rivers: Bighorn River, Cheyenne River, Green River, North Platte River, Powder River, Snake River, Yellowstone River

Major bodies of water: Alcova Reservoir, Boysen Reservoir, Buffalo Bill Reservoir, Flaming Gorge Reservoir, Fremont Lake, Glendo Reservoir, Guernsey Reservoir, Jackson Lake, Keyhole Reservoir, Pathfinder Reservoir, Seminoe Reservoir, Shoshone Lake, Yellowstone Lake

Climate: In January temperatures range from 8°F (-13°C) to 31°F (-1°C), and in July temperatures range from 56°F (13°C) to 86°F (30°C). Throughout the year, temperatures in the mountains are cooler than at lower elevations. The average yearly precipitation is 13 inches (33 cm).

Resources, industries, and products: Mineral extraction, tourism and recreation, refined petroleum products, foods, wood products, stone, clay and glass products, wheat, beans, oats, sugar beets, cattle, coal

History: The United States bought most of the Wyoming region in 1803 as part of the Louisiana Purchase. John Colter explored the area in 1807 and discovered the Yellowstone geysers and hot springs. The Territory of Wyoming was created in 1868, and in 1890 Wyoming became the forty-fourth state.

Historic sites and other attractions: Yellowstone National Park, Grand Teton National Park, Devils Tower National Monument, Fort Laramie National Historic Site, Fossil Butte National Monument, Wind River Canyon

Unusual facts: Wyoming Territory was the first place in the United States to grant women the right to vote. Because of Wyoming's history of equal rights for women, it is nicknamed the Equality State. Wyoming was the first state to elect a woman governor—Nellie Tayloe Ross was elected in 1924. Yellowstone, established in 1872, is the nation's oldest national park.

Original American Indian groups: Arapaho, Crow, Northern Shoshoni

Harcourt Brace School Publishers

Name _____

Harcourt Brace School Publishers

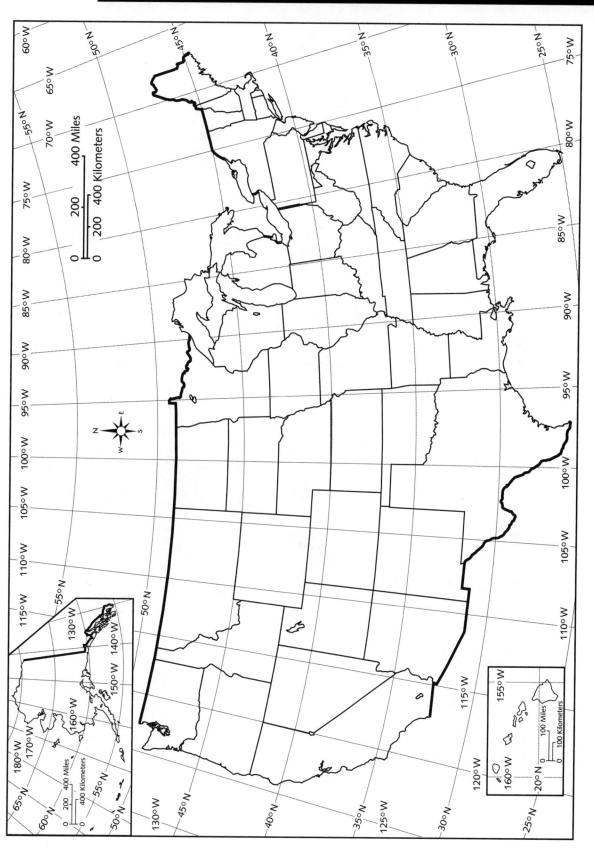

THE MAP BOOK

*T*HE *U*NITED *S*TATES–*P*HYSICAL

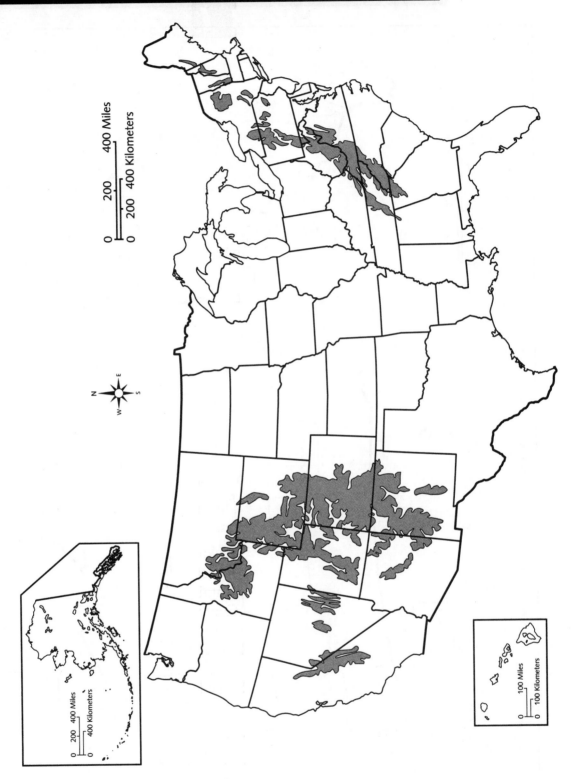

Harcourt Brace School Publishers

THE MAP BOOK

Name _____

State population rank:

1 California	18 Wisconsin	35 West Virginia
2 Texas	19 Maryland	36 New Mexico
3 New York	20 Minnesota	37 Nebraska
4 Florida	21 Louisiana	38 Nevada
5 Pennsylvania	22 Alabama	39 Maine
6 Illinois	23 Arizona	40 Hawaii
7 Ohio	24 Kentucky	41 New Hampshire
8 Michigan	25 South Carolina	42 Idaho
9 New Jersey	26 Colorado	43 Rhode Island
10 North Carolina	27 Connecticut	44 Montana
11 Georgia	28 Oklahoma	45 South Dakota
12 Virginia	29 Oregon	46 Delaware
13 Massachusetts	30 Iowa	47 North Dakota
14 Indiana	31 Mississippi	48 Alaska
15 Washington	32 Kansas	49 Vermont
16 Missouri	33 Arkansas	50 Wyoming
17 Tennessee	34 Utah	

Total population (including Washington, D.C., and Puerto Rico): 270,932,000

Largest cities: New York City, Los Angeles, Chicago, Houston, Philadelphia, San Diego, Detroit, Dallas, Phoenix, San Antonio

Major land areas: Adirondack Mountains, Alaska Range, Appalachian Mountains, Appalachian Plateau, Arctic Coastal Plain, Atlantic Coastal Plain, Basin and Range Region, Blue Ridge Mountains, Brooks Range, Cascade Range, Central Lowlands and Uplands, Central Plains, Central Valley, Coast Ranges, Colorado Plateau, Columbia Plateau, Great Plains, Gulf Coastal Plain, Hawaii, Imperial Valley, Interior Low Plateau, Kahoolawe, Kauai, Lanai, Maui, Molokai, New England Upland, Niihau, Oahu, Ouachita Mountains, Ozark Plateau, Piedmont, Rocky Mountains, Sierra Nevada, Superior Upland, Wyoming Basin

Lowest point: Death Valley in California, 282 feet (86 m) below sea level

Highest point: Mount McKinley in Alaska, 20,320 feet (6,194 m)

Major rivers: Alabama River, Arkansas River, Brazos River, Colorado River, Columbia River, Connecticut River, Delaware River, Hudson River, James River, Mississippi River, Missouri River, Potomac River, Red River, Rio Grande, Sacramento River, San Joaquin River, Susquehanna River, Yukon River

Continued on page 108.

Harcourt Brace School Publishers

THE MAP BOOK

Name _____

Major bodies of water: Chesapeake Bay, Delaware Bay, Great Salt Lake, Lake Erie, Lake Huron, Iliamna Lake, Lake Michigan, Lake of the Woods, Lake Okeechobee, Lake Ontario, Lake Superior, Lake Tahoe, Mobile Bay, Monterey Bay, Puget Sound

Climate: The United States has a broad range of climates, varying from the tropical climates of Hawaii and southern Florida to the subarctic climate of Alaska. The Southeast states have a subtropical climate with a lot of precipitation. The Northeast states have a mild climate with moderate precipitation. Farther west is the semiarid (steppe) climate of the Great Plains. The climate in the Southwest is arid. The hottest and driest places in the country are in the Southwest. On the Pacific coast, it is subtropical in southern California and mild from northern California to southeastern Alaska. The Pacific Northwest is one of the wettest places in the country.

Resources, industries, and products: Aircraft, iron and steel products, machinery, metal products, paper products, textiles, transportation equipment, aluminum, coal, copper, iron ore, lead, natural gas, oil, silver, zinc, cattle, hogs, sheep, dairy products, cotton, barley, wheat, corn, oats, fruit, soybeans, sugar, vegetables

History: Exploration began after Columbus sighted the Bahamas in 1492. The first Europeans to settle in what is now the United States were the Spanish. They built St. Augustine in Florida. English settlers started Jamestown in 1607. Soon many settlements began along the Atlantic coast. Most of these settlements were controlled by England. In the late 1700s Britain began asking for taxes that the Americans thought were unfair. This set off the American Revolution (1775–1783). The United States declared its independence on July 4, 1776. After the Revolution, United States citizens adopted the Constitution and elected George Washington as their first President. The country began to grow westward. In 1783 our western border was the Mississippi River. By 1850 the western border was the Pacific Ocean. The new states forming in the West had many links to the North. Southern leaders were afraid of losing power in the government. When Abraham Lincoln was elected President, the South withdrew from the Union. Civil War broke out in 1861. The war ended in 1865, and the United States remained one nation. Russia sold Alaska to the United States for $7.2 million in 1867. In 1959 Hawaii became the fiftieth state.

Major explorers: Sebastian Cabot, Ponce de León, Francisco de Coronado, Giovanni da Verrazano, Jacques Cartier, Hernando de Soto, Francis Drake, Samuel de Champlain, John Smith, Henry Hudson, Jacques Marquette, Louis Joliet, Robert de La Salle, James Cook, Meriwether Lewis and William Clark, Zebulon Pike, John Fremont, John W. Powell

THE MAP BOOK

Name _____

UNITED STATES–REGIONS

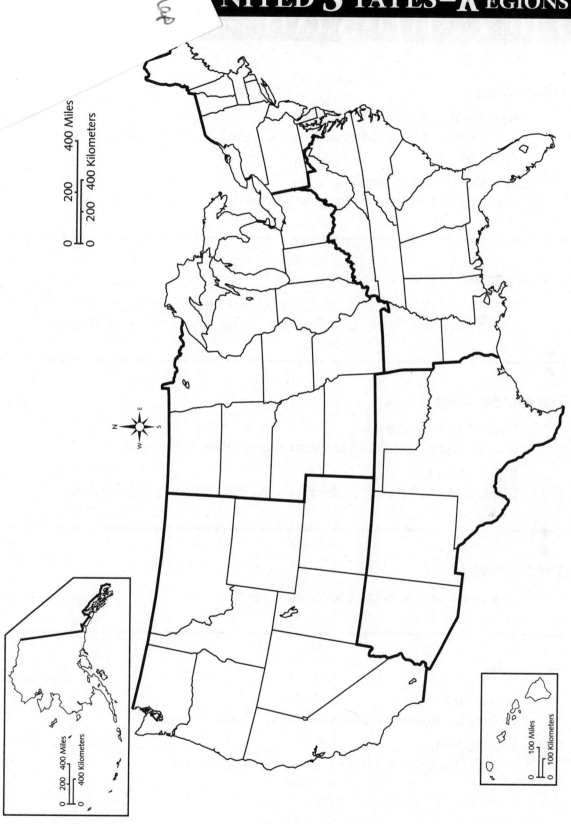

400 Miles

200   400 Kilometers

0   200   400

200   400 Miles

0   200   400 Kilometers

100 Miles

0   100 Kilometers

THE MAP BOOK

FACTS ABOUT
THE UNITED STATES—REGIONS

The Northeast

New England States:
Connecticut, Maine, Massachusetts, New Hampshire, Rhode Island, Vermont

Middle Atlantic States:
Delaware, Maryland, New Jersey, New York, Pennsylvania

The Southeast

Alabama, Arkansas, Florida, Georgia, Kentucky, Louisiana, Mississippi, North Carolina, South Carolina, Tennessee, Virginia, West Virginia

The Middle West

Great Lakes States:
Illinois, Indiana, Michigan, Minnesota, Ohio, Wisconsin

Plains States:
Iowa, Kansas, Missouri, Nebraska, North Dakota, South Dakota

The Southwest

Arizona, New Mexico, Oklahoma, Texas

The West

Mountain States:
Colorado, Idaho, Montana, Nevada, Utah, Wyoming

Pacific States:
Alaska, California, Hawaii, Oregon, Washington

Harcourt Brace School Publishers

THE MAP BOOK

Name _____

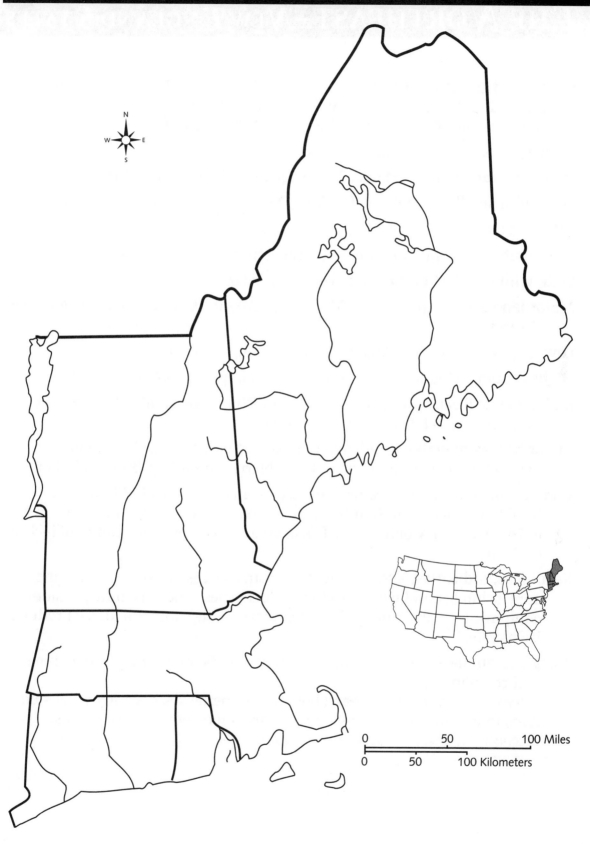

Harcourt Brace School Publishers

0   50   100 Miles
0   50   100 Kilometers

Name _____

THE NORTHEAST–NEW ENGLAND STATES

States (and ✪capital cities): Connecticut (✪Hartford), Maine (✪Augusta), Massachusetts (✪Boston), New Hampshire (✪Concord), Rhode Island (✪Providence), Vermont (✪Montpelier)

Total area: 62,811 square miles (162,668 sq km)

State with largest area: Maine, 30,865 square miles (79,940 sq km)

State with smallest area: Rhode Island, 1,045 square miles (2,706 sq km)

Total population: 13,379,000

State with largest population: Massachusetts, 6,118,000

State with smallest population: Vermont, 588,000

Major land areas: Appalachian Mountains, Atlantic Coastal Plain, New England Upland

Lowest point: Along the Atlantic Coastal Plain, sea level

Highest point: Mount Washington in New Hampshire, 6,288 feet (1,917 m)

Major rivers: Blackstone River, Connecticut River, Housatonic River, Kennebec River, Merrimack River, Penobscot River

Major bodies of water: Candlewood Lake (artificial), Lake Champlain, Massachusetts Bay, Moosehead Lake, Narragansett Bay, Boston Harbor

Climate: In January temperatures average from 15°F (–9°C) in Maine to 25°F (–4°C) in Connecticut. In July temperatures average from 68°F (20°C) in Maine to 74°F (23°C) in Connecticut. The average yearly precipitation is 40 inches (102 cm).

Resources, industries, and products: Christmas trees, mushrooms, fishing, apples, lumber and wood products, blueberries, chickens, transportation equipment, printing and publishing, maple syrup, tourism, dairy products, jewelry, textiles

Trees and animals: *Trees*—beech, birch, cedar, fir, hemlock, maple, oak, pine, spruce, tulip tree
Animals—beavers, black bears, bobcats, copperheads, deer, foxes, lobsters, lynx, minks, moose, muskrats, opossums, otters, porcupines, rabbits, raccoons, skunks, squirrels, woodchucks

Name _____

Harcourt Brace School Publishers

0   50   100 Miles

0   50   100 Kilometers

FACTS ABOUT
THE NORTHEAST–MIDDLE ATLANTIC STATES

States (and ✪capital cities): Delaware (✪Dover), Maryland (✪Annapolis), New Jersey (✪Trenton), New York (✪Albany), Pennsylvania (✪Harrisburg)

Total area: 111,193 square miles (287,990 sq km)

State with largest area: New York, 47,224 square miles (122,310 sq km)

State with smallest area: Delaware, 1,955 square miles (5,063 sq km)

Total population: 44,036,000

State with largest population: New York, 18,137,000

State with smallest population: Delaware, 731,000

Major land areas: Allegheny Mountains, Appalachian Mountains, Adirondack Mountains, Appalachian Plateau, Atlantic Coastal Plain, Catskill Mountains, Pocono Mountains

Lowest point: Along the Atlantic Coastal Plain, sea level

Highest point: Mount Marcy in New York, 5,344 feet (1,629 m)

Major rivers: Allegheny River, Delaware River, Hudson River, Ohio River, Monongahela River, Potomac River, St. Lawrence River, Susquehanna River

Major bodies of water: Chesapeake Bay, Delaware Bay, Finger Lakes, Lake Erie, Lake Ontario, New York Bay, Niagara Falls

Climate: In January temperatures average from 23 °F (–5 °C) in New York to 32 °F (0 °C) in Maryland. In July temperatures average from 72 °F (22 °C) in New York to 77 °F (25 °C) in Maryland. The average yearly precipitation is 40 inches (102 cm).

Resources, industries, and products: Chemicals, soybeans, corn, fishing, tourism, electrical machinery, stone, cranberries, toys and sporting goods, milk, cheese, wine, communications, steel, coal, mushrooms, hay, metals

Trees and animals: *Trees*—beech, birch, cedar, fir, hemlock, maple, oak, pine, spruce, tulip tree
Animals—beavers, black bears, bobcats, copperheads, deer, foxes, lynx, minks, moose, muskrats, opossums, otters, porcupines, rabbits, raccoons, skunks, squirrels, woodchucks

Name _____

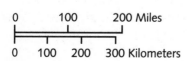

Harcourt Brace School Publishers

0   100   200 Miles

0   100   200   300 Kilometers

Name _____

States (and ✪capital cities): Alabama (✪Montgomery), Arkansas (✪Little Rock), Florida (✪Tallahassee), Georgia (✪Atlanta), Kentucky (✪Frankfort), Louisiana (✪Baton Rouge), Mississippi (✪Jackson), North Carolina (✪Raleigh), South Carolina (✪Columbia), Tennessee (✪Nashville), Virginia (✪Richmond), West Virginia (✪Charleston)

Total area: 533,091 square miles (1,380,706 sq km)

State with largest area: Georgia, 58,876 square miles (152,489 sq km)

State with smallest area: South Carolina, 31,055 square miles (80,432 sq km)

Total population: 65,076,000

State with largest population: Florida, 14,653,000

State with smallest population: West Virginia, 1,815,000

Major land areas: Appalachian Mountains, Appalachian Plateau, Atlantic Coastal Plain, Blue Ridge Mountains, Gulf Coastal Plain, Interior Low Plateau, Ouachita Mountains, Ozark Plateau, Piedmont

Lowest point: New Orleans, Louisiana, 5 feet (1.5 m) below sea level

Highest point: Mount Mitchell in North Carolina, 6,684 feet (2,037 m)

Major rivers: Alabama R., Altamaha R., Arkansas R., Chattahoochee R., Flint R., Kentucky R., Mississippi R., Mobile R., Ohio R., Pearl R., Potomac R., Red R., Roanoke R., Sabine R., Savannah R., Tennessee R., Tombigbee R.

Major bodies of water: Albemarle Sound, Chesapeake Bay, Guntersville Lake (artificial), Kentucky Lake (artificial), Kerr Reservoir, Lake Cumberland, Lake Okeechobee, Lake Ouachita, Lake Pontchartrain, Lake Seminole, Mobile Bay, Pamlico Sound, Roanoke Rapids (artificial)

Climate: In January temperatures average from 33°F (1°C) in West Virginia to 67°F (19°C) in Florida. In July temperatures average 83°F (28°C) in Florida and become cooler as you travel north. The average yearly precipitation is 46 inches (117 cm), but there can be up to 100 inches (254 cm) in some areas.

Resources, industries, and products: Textiles, chemicals, paper products, furniture, processed foods, electrical equipment, shipbuilding, coal, iron, oil, natural gas, lumber, fishing, cattle, hogs, poultry, dairy products, cotton, soybeans, peanuts, corn, rice, apples, oranges, sugarcane, tomatoes, tourism

Trees and animals: *Trees*—ash, bald cyprus, bay, beech, fir, gum, hickory, maple, oak, pine, spruce, tulip tree, palm
Animals—alligators, bears, beavers, bobcats, deer, Florida panthers, foxes, minks, muskrats, opossums, rabbits, raccoons, skunks, squirrels, weasels, wild hogs, wild turkeys, woodchucks

Harcourt Brace School Publishers

THE MIDDLE WEST–GREAT LAKES STATES

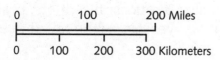

FACTS ABOUT
THE MIDDLE WEST–GREAT LAKES STATES

States (and ✪capital cities): Illinois (✪Springfield), Indiana (✪Indianapolis), Michigan (✪Lansing), Minnesota (✪St. Paul), Ohio (✪Columbus), Wisconsin (✪Madison)

Total area: 332,351 square miles (860,789 sq km)

State with largest area: Minnesota, 84,068 square miles (217,736 sq km)

State with smallest area: Indiana, 36,291 square miles (93,994 sq km)

Total population: 48,576,000

State with largest population: Illinois, 11,895,000

State with smallest population: Minnesota, 4,685,000

Major land areas: Appalachian Plateau, Central Plains, Interior Low Plateau, Superior Upland

Lowest point: Along the Mississippi River in Illinois, 279 feet (85 m) above sea level

Highest point: Eagle Mountain in Minnesota, 2,301 feet (701 m)

Major rivers: Black River, Des Moines River, Grand River, Illinois River, Maumee River, Menominee River, Minnesota River, Mississippi River, Montreal River, Muskegon River, Ohio River, Red River of the North, St. Croix River, Scioto River, Wabash River, White River, Wisconsin River

Major bodies of water: Green Lake, Houghton Lake, Lake Erie, Lake Huron, Lake Itasca, Lake Michigan, Lake of the Woods, Lake Saint Clair, Lake Superior, Lake Wawasee, Leech Lake, Mille Lacs Lake, Minnehaha Falls, Red Lake, Saginaw Bay

Climate: In January temperatures average from 2°F (–17°C) in upper Minnesota to 36°F (2°C) in southern Illinois. In July temperatures average from 68°F (20°C) in upper Minnesota to 79°F (26°C) in Illinois. The climate gets warmer as you travel south in the Great Lakes region. The average yearly precipitation is 33 inches (84 cm).

Resources, industries, and products: Transportation equipment, machinery, metals, processed foods, meat packing, electronic equipment, chemicals, paper and paper products, book publishing, coal, iron ore, copper, oil, fishing, cattle, hogs, poultry, dairy products, corn, hay, wheat, soybeans, oats, tourism

Trees and animals: *Trees*—aspen, basswood, beech, fir, hemlock, hickory, larch, maple, oak, pine, spruce, yellow birch
Animals—badgers, beavers, black bears, bobcats, Canada geese, coyotes, gray and red foxes, gophers, moose, muskrats, opossums, otters, prairie mice, rabbits, raccoons, squirrels, striped skunks, weasels, white-tailed deer, woodchucks

Harcourt Brace School Publishers

THE MAP BOOK

Name _____

Harcourt Brace School Publishers

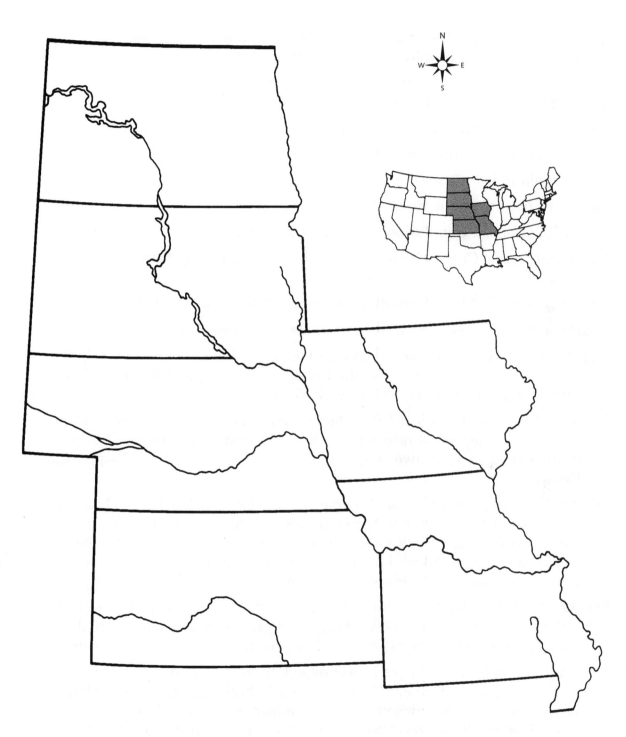

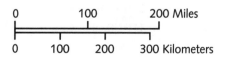

Name _____

States (and ✪capital cities): Iowa (✪Des Moines), Kansas (✪Topeka), Missouri (✪Jefferson City), Nebraska (✪Lincoln), North Dakota (✪Bismarck), South Dakota (✪Pierre)

Total area: 433,179 square miles (1,121,934 sq km)

State with largest area: Kansas, 82,264 square miles (213,064 sq km)

State with smallest area: Iowa, 56,290 square miles (145,791 sq km)

Total population: 13,885,000

State with largest population: Missouri, 5,402,000

State with smallest population: North Dakota, 640,000

Major land areas: Central Plains, Great Plains, Interior Low Plateau, Ozark Plateau

Lowest point: The Mississippi River in Iowa, 480 feet (146 m) above sea level

Highest point: Harney Peak in South Dakota, 7,242 feet (2,207 m)

Major rivers: Arkansas River, Big Sioux River, Des Moines River, Mississippi River, Missouri River, North Platte River, Platte River, Red River, St. Francis River, South Platte River, Yellowstone River

Major bodies of water: Clear Lake, Devils Lake, Lake Francis Case (artificial), Lake McConaughy (artificial), Lake Oahe (artificial), Lake of the Ozarks (artificial), Lake Sakakawea (artificial), Milford Lake (artificial), Wappapello Reservoir

Climate: In January temperatures average from 3°F (–16°C) in North Dakota to 32°F (0°C) in Kansas. In July temperatures average from 69°F (21°C) in North Dakota to 79°F (26°C) in Kansas. The average yearly precipitation in North Dakota and South Dakota is 18 inches (46 cm). The average yearly precipitation in the rest of the Plains states is 34 inches (86 cm).

Resources, industries, and products: Transportation equipment, chemicals, book publishing, machinery, meat packing, food processing, metals, oil, coal, gold, cattle, pigs, sheep, dairy products, wheat, corn, soybeans, oats, tourism

Trees and animals: *Trees*—aspen, cottonwood, hickory, oak, pine, willow *Animals*—badgers, beavers, bighorn sheep, bobcats, buffaloes, cottontail rabbits, coyotes, elks, flickertail ground squirrels, foxes, jackrabbits, lynx, mule deer, muskrats, opossums, prairie dogs, pronghorn antelopes, rabbits, raccoons, skunks, squirrels, weasels, white-tailed deer

Name _____

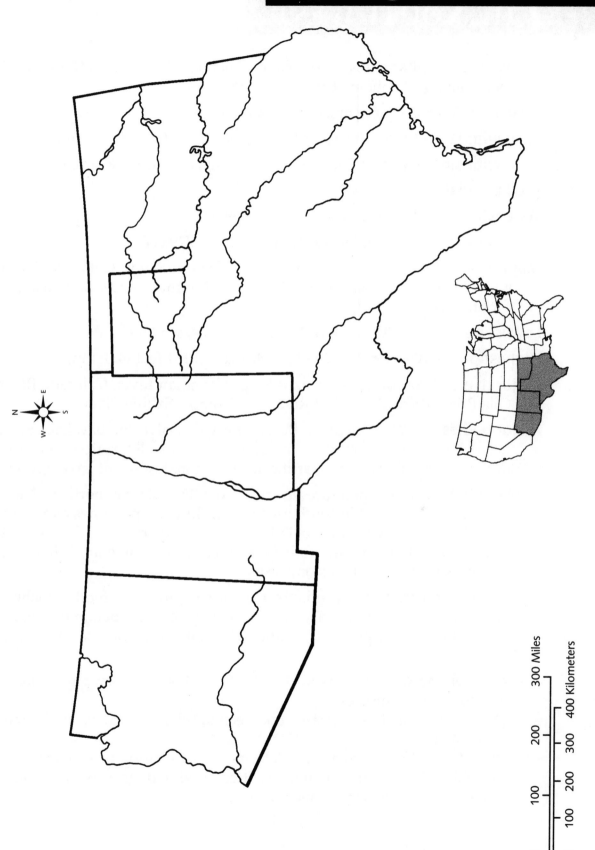

Harcourt Brace School Publishers

300 Miles

400 Kilometers

200

300

200

100

200

100

100

0

0

FACTS ABOUT
THE SOUTHWEST

States (and ✪capital cities): Arizona (✪Phoenix), New Mexico (✪Santa Fe), Oklahoma (✪Oklahoma City), Texas (✪Austin)

Total area: 572,832 square miles (1,483,635 sq km)

State with largest area: Texas, 267,338 square miles (692,405 sq km)

State with smallest area: Oklahoma, 69,919 square miles (181,090 sq km)

Total population: 29,041,000

State with largest population: Texas, 19,439,000

State with smallest population: New Mexico, 1,729,000

Major land areas: Basin and Range Region, Central Plains, Colorado Plateau, Great Plains, Gulf Coastal Plain, Ouachita Mountains, Ozark Plateau, Rocky Mountains

Lowest point: Along the Gulf of Mexico in Texas, sea level

Highest point: Wheeler Peak in New Mexico, 13,161 feet (4,011 m)

Major rivers: Arkansas River, Brazos River, Canadian River, Colorado River, Gila River, Pecos River, Red River, Rio Grande, Sabine River

Major bodies of water: Elephant Butte Reservoir, Galveston Bay, Lake Mead (artificial), Lake O'The Cherokees (artificial), Lake Powell (artificial), Lake Texoma (artificial), San Carlos Lake (artificial), Theodore Roosevelt Lake (artificial)

Climate: In January temperatures average from 35°F (2°C) in northern New Mexico to 60°F (16°C) in southern Texas. In July temperatures average from 74°F (23°C) in New Mexico to 85°F (29°C) in southern Texas. The average yearly precipitation varies from 7 inches (18 cm) in Phoenix, Arizona, to 48 inches (122 cm) in Houston, Texas.

Resources, industries, and products: Chemicals, processed foods, machinery, electronic equipment, metals, oil, coal, natural gas, copper, uranium, fishing, cattle, sheep, dairy products, cotton, wheat, hay, rice, carrots, onions, spinach, melons, tourism

Trees and animals: *Trees*—aspen, Douglas fir, hickory, juniper, piñon, ponderosa pine, scrub oak, spruce
Shrubs—creosote bush, greasewood, lechuquilla, sagebrush, sotol, saguaro cactus, yucca
Animals—badgers, beavers, black bears, bobcats, chipmunks, coyotes, foxes, jackrabbits, minks, mountain lions, otters, prairie dogs, pronghorn antelopes, raccoons, squirrels, white-tailed deer

Name _____

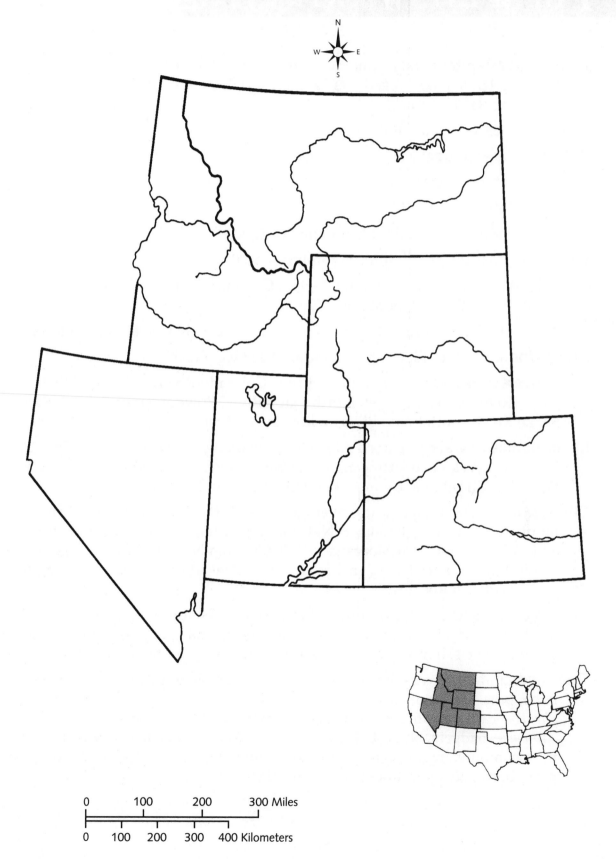

0	100	200	300 Miles

0	100	200	300	400 Kilometers

Name _____

FACTS ABOUT

THE WEST–MOUNTAIN STATES

States (and ✪capital cities): Colorado (✪Denver), Idaho (✪Boise), Montana (✪Helena), Nevada (✪Carson City), Utah (✪Salt Lake City), Wyoming (✪Cheyenne)

Total area: 628,312 square miles (1,627,328 sq km)

State with largest area: Montana, 147,138 square miles (381,087 sq km)

State with smallest area: Idaho, 83,557 square miles (216,412 sq km)

Total population: 10,197,000

State with largest population: Colorado, 3,892,000

State with smallest population: Wyoming, 479,000

Major land areas: Basin and Range Region, Colorado Plateau, Columbia Plateau, Great Plains, Rocky Mountains, Wyoming Basin

Lowest point: The Colorado River in Nevada, 470 feet (143 m) above sea level

Highest point: Mount Elbert in Colorado, 14,433 feet (4,399 m)

Major rivers: Arkansas River, Bighorn River, Colorado River, Columbia River, Green River, Missouri River, North Platte River, Powder River, Salmon River, Snake River, South Platte River, Yellowstone River

Major bodies of water: Coeur d'Alene Lake, Flaming Gorge Reservoir, Flathead Lake, Fort Peck Lake (artificial), Great Salt Lake, Lake Mead (artificial), Lake Powell (artificial), Lake Tahoe, Pend Oreille Lake, Yellowstone Lake

Climate: In January temperatures average from 10°F (–12°C) in the northern mountain areas to 43°F (6°C) in Nevada. In July temperatures average from 60°F (16°C) in northern Montana to 86°F (30°C) in Nevada. The average yearly precipitation ranges from 7 inches (18 cm) in Nevada to 50 inches (127 cm) in the northern Rockies.

Resources, industries, and products: Processed foods, lumber and wood products, lead, zinc, copper, silver, gold, coal, oil, natural gas, cattle, sheep, dairy products, hay, wheat, corn, barley, sugar beets, potatoes, tourism

Trees and animals: *Trees*—aspen, cottonwood, Douglas fir, hemlock, juniper, larch, pine, spruce, willow
Shrubs—cacti, ocotillo, paloverde, sagebrush, shadscale
Animals—badgers, bears, bobcats, cougars, coyotes, elks, foxes, lynx, martens, moose, mountain goats, mountain lions, mule deer, muskrats, prairie dogs, pronghorn antelopes, Rocky Mountain sheep

Harcourt Brace School Publishers

THE MAP BOOK

Name _____

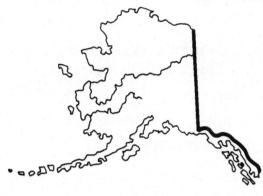

0   500 Miles

0   250 500 Kilometers

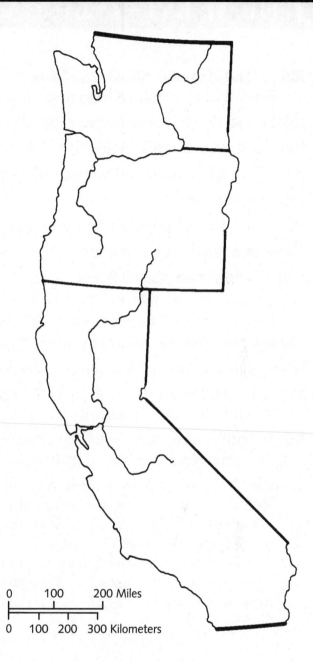

0   100   200 Miles

0   100   200   300 Kilometers

N
W   E
S

0   100   200 Miles

0   100 200 300 Kilometers

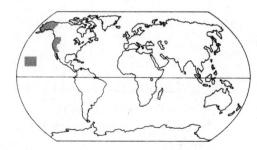

Harcourt Brace School Publishers

FACTS ABOUT
THE WEST–PACIFIC STATES

States (and ⚙ capital cities): Alaska (⚙ Juneau), California (⚙ Sacramento), Hawaii (⚙ Honolulu), Oregon (⚙ Salem), Washington (⚙ Olympia)

Total area: 920,073 square miles (2,382,989 sq km)

State with largest area: Alaska, 589,757 square miles (1,527,470 sq km)

State with smallest area: Hawaii, 6,450 square miles (16,705 sq km)

Total population: 42,918,000

State with largest population: California, 32,268,000

State with smallest population: Alaska, 609,000

Major land areas: Alaska Range, Arctic Plains, Basin and Range Region, Brooks Range, Cascade Range, Central Lowlands and Uplands, Central Valley, Coast Ranges, Columbia Plateau, Imperial Valley, Rocky Mountains, Sierra Nevada

Lowest point: Death Valley in California, 282 feet (86 m) below sea level

Highest point: Mount McKinley in Alaska, 20,320 feet (6,194 m)

Major rivers: Columbia River, Kuskokwim River, Sacramento River, San Joaquin River, Willamette River, Yukon River

Major bodies of water: Crater Lake, Iliamna Lake, Lake Tahoe, Monterey Bay, Pearl Harbor, Puget Sound, Salton Sea, San Francisco Bay, Shasta Lake

Climate: In January temperatures average from 25°F (–4°C) in Washington to 55°F (13°C) in California. In July temperatures average from 70°F (21°C) in Washington to 73°F (23°C) in California. The average yearly precipitation ranges from 10 inches (25 cm) in California to as much as 135 inches (343 cm) in Washington. In Alaska, January temperatures average from –11°F (–24°C) in the Arctic to 28°F (–2°C) in the south. Alaska's July temperatures average from 47°F (8°C) to 55°F (13°C). Alaska's yearly precipitation varies from 4 inches (10 cm) to 20 inches (51 cm). In Hawaii, temperatures average 71°F (22°C) in January and 77°F (25°C) in July. Hawaii's yearly precipitation varies from 10 inches (25 cm) to 300 inches (762 cm).

Resources, industries, and products: Paper products, jet airplanes, film production, oil, fishing, cattle, dairy products, hay, wheat, vegetables, cherries, apples, berries, pineapples, sugarcane, coffee, tourism

Trees and animals: *Trees*—Douglas fir, hemlock, juniper, koa, larch, oak, palm, pine, redwood, spruce
Animals—antelopes, bears, deer, dolphins, elks, foxes, minks, mountain goats, musk oxen, seals, wildcats, wolverines

Harcourt Brace School Publishers

THE MAP BOOK

Name _____

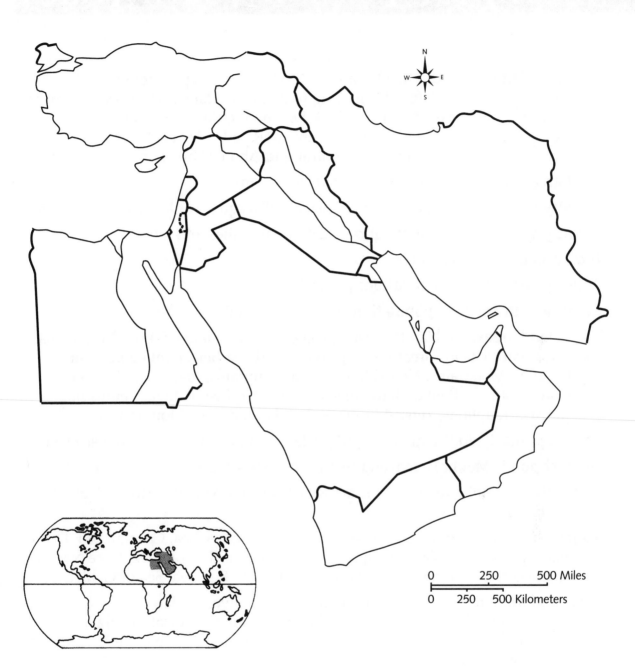

0   250   500 Miles

0   250   500 Kilometers

Harcourt Brace School Publishers

Name _____

FACTS ABOUT
SOUTHWEST ASIA AND NORTH AFRICA

Countries (and ✪capital cities): Bahrain (✪Manama), Cyprus (✪Nicosia), Egypt (✪Cairo), Iran (✪Tehran), Iraq (✪Baghdad), Israel (✪Jerusalem), Jordan (✪Amman), Kuwait (✪Kuwait City), Lebanon (✪Beirut), Oman (✪Muscat), Qatar (✪Doha), Saudi Arabia (✪Riyadh), Syria (✪Damascus), Turkey (✪Ankara), United Arab Emirates (✪Abu Dhabi), Yemen (✪Sanaa)

Total area: 2,838,029 square miles (7,350,495 sq km)

Country with largest area: Saudi Arabia, 865,000 square miles (2,240,350 sq km)

Country with smallest area: Bahrain, 268 square miles (694 sq km)

Total population: 290,621,000

Country with largest population: Iran, 67,540,000

Country with smallest population: Bahrain, 604,000

Major land areas: Arabian Peninsula, Caucasus Mountains, Elburz Mountains, Gilf Kebir Plateau, Great Kavir, Jordan-Dead Sea-Bekáa Valley Lowland, Lebanon Mountains, Nile Valley, Oman Mountains, Plateau of Anatolia, Plateau of Iran, Pontic Mountains, Qattara Depression, Sinai Peninsula, Taurus Mountains, Tigris-Euphrates Lowland, Zagros Mountains

Lowest point: Dead Sea in Israel and Jordan, 1,312 feet (400 m) below sea level

Highest point: Mount Damavand in Turkey, 18,934 feet (5,771 m)

Major rivers: Euphrates River, Jordan River, Karun River, Nile River, Shatt al Arab, Tigris River

Major bodies of water: Aegean Sea, Arabian Sea, Black Sea, Caspian Sea, Dead Sea, Gulf of Aden, Gulf of Aqaba, Gulf of Oman, Gulf of Suez, Lake Nasser (artificial), Lake Urmia, Lake Van, Persian Gulf, Red Sea, Sea of Galilee

Trees and animals: *Trees*—ash, beech, date palm, olive, poplar *Animals*—antelopes, Arabian oryx, badgers, camels, caracals, cobras, crocodiles, dromedaries, ibexes, leopards, lions, onagers, panthers, wild boars, wolves, zebu oxen

Harcourt Brace School Publishers

128   THE MAP BOOK

Name _____

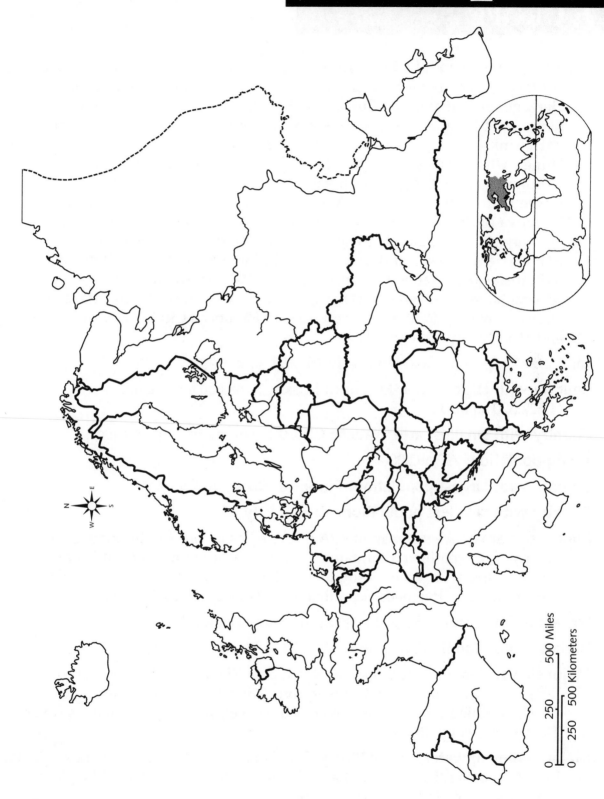

Harcourt Brace School Publishers

500 Miles

500 Kilometers

250

250

0

0

FACTS ABOUT
*E*UROPE

Countries (and ✪capital cities): Albania (✪Tiranë), Andorra (✪Andorra la Vella), Austria (✪Vienna), Belarus (✪Minsk), Belgium (✪Brussels), Bosnia and Herzegovina (✪Sarajevo), Bulgaria (✪Sofia), Croatia (✪Zagreb), Czech Republic (✪Prague), Denmark (✪Copenhagen), Estonia (✪Tallinn), Finland (✪Helsinki), France (✪Paris), Germany (✪Berlin), Greece (✪Athens), Hungary (✪Budapest), Iceland (✪Reykjavik), Ireland (✪Dublin), Italy (✪Rome), Latvia (✪Riga), Liechtenstein (✪Vaduz), Lithuania (✪Vilnius), Luxembourg (✪Luxembourg), Macedonia (✪Skopje), Malta (✪Valletta), Moldova (✪Chisinau), Monaco (✪Monaco), Netherlands (✪Amsterdam), Norway (✪Oslo), Poland (✪Warsaw), Portugal (✪Lisbon), Romania (✪Bucharest), Russia (✪Moscow), San Marino (✪San Marino), Slovakia (✪Bratislava), Slovenia (✪Ljubljana), Spain (✪Madrid), Sweden (✪Stockholm), Switzerland (✪Bern), Turkey (✪Ankara), Ukraine (✪Kiev), United Kingdom (✪London), Vatican City (✪Vatican City), Yugoslavia: Serbia and Montenegro (✪Belgrade)

Total area: 4,036,100 square miles (10,452,691 sq km)

Country with largest area: European Russia, 1,748,000 square miles (4,527,320 sq km)

Country with smallest area: Vatican City, 0.17 square mile (0.44 sq km)

Total population: 792,692,000

Country with largest population: European Russia, 147,987,000

Country with smallest population: Vatican City, 771

Major land areas: Alps, Apennines, Aquitaine Basin, Balkan Mountains, Balkan Peninsula, Carpathian Mountains, Caucasus Mountains, Central Uplands, Dinaric Alps, Hungarian Basin, Iberian Peninsula, Italian Peninsula, North European Plain, Pyrenees, Scandinavian Peninsula, Ural Mountains

Lowest point: Caspian Sea, 92 feet (28 m) below sea level

Highest point: Mount El'brus in Russia, 18,510 feet (5,642 m)

Major rivers: Danube River, Dneiper River, Don River, Douro River, Ebro River, Elbe River, Garonne River, Guadalquivir River, Loire River, Oder River, Po River, Rhine River, Rhone River, Seine River, Tagus River, Thames River, Tiber River, Volga River

Major bodies of water: Bay of Biscay, Caspian Sea, English Channel, Lake Como, Lake Constance, Lake Garda, Lake Geneva, Lake Ladoga, Lake Maggiore, Lake Neuchâtel, Lake Onega, Lake Scutari

Harcourt Brace School Publishers

Name _____

0   50   100 Miles

0   50   100 150 Kilometers

Harcourt Brace School Publishers

Name _____

FACTS ABOUT
THE BRITISH ISLES

Countries (and ⊙capital cities): Ireland (⊙Dublin),
United Kingdom of Great Britain and Northern Ireland (⊙London)

Total area: 121,388 square miles (314,394 sq km)

Lands included in the United Kingdom of Great Britain and Northern Ireland:
Great Britain is composed of England (⊙London), Scotland (⊙Edinburgh), and Wales (⊙Cardiff). Northern Ireland comprises six of the nine counties of Ulster (⊙Belfast).

Total population: 62,166,000

Country with largest population: United Kingdom of Great Britain and Northern Ireland 58,135,000

Country with smallest population: Ireland, 3,556,000

Major land areas: Cambrian Mountains, Central Lowlands, Central Plain, Cheviot Hills, Coastal Highlands, Cotswold Hills, Downs, The Fens, Grampian Mountains, Lake District, Midlands (East and West), Mountains of Kerry, Mourne Mountains, Munster Range, Northwest Highlands, Pennine Chain, Southern Uplands, Wicklow Mountains

Lowest point: Along the coasts, sea level

Highest point: Ben Nevis in Scotland, 4,406 feet (1,343 m)

Major rivers: Avon River, Bann River, Barrow River, Blackwater River, Boyne River, Clyde River, Dee River, Exe River, Humber River, Liffey River, Mersey River, Nore River, Ouse River, Severn River, Shannon River, Slaney River, Teifi River, Thames River, Trent River, Tweed River, Tyne River, Wye River

Major bodies of water: Bristol Channel, Cardigan Bay, Donegal Bay, English Channel, Firth of Clyde, Firth of Forth, Galway Bay, Irish Sea, Lake Corrib, Lake Foyle, Lake Neagh, Loch Lomond, Loch Ness, Moray Firth, North Channel, North Sea, St. George's Channel, Solway Firth, Strait of Dover, Tralee Bay, The Wash

Resources, industries, and products: Potatoes, dairy products, wool, fishing, chemicals, coal, steel, mining, electronics, motor vehicles, shipbuilding, banking, textiles, clothing, brewing, tourism, grain, zinc, sugar beets, tin

Unusual facts: The 0° meridian of longitude passes through the Royal Observatory, Greenwich, in Greater London. Big Ben, the bell in the clock tower of the House of Parliament, weighs $13\frac{1}{2}$ short tons (12 metric tons).

Harcourt Brace School Publishers

Name _____

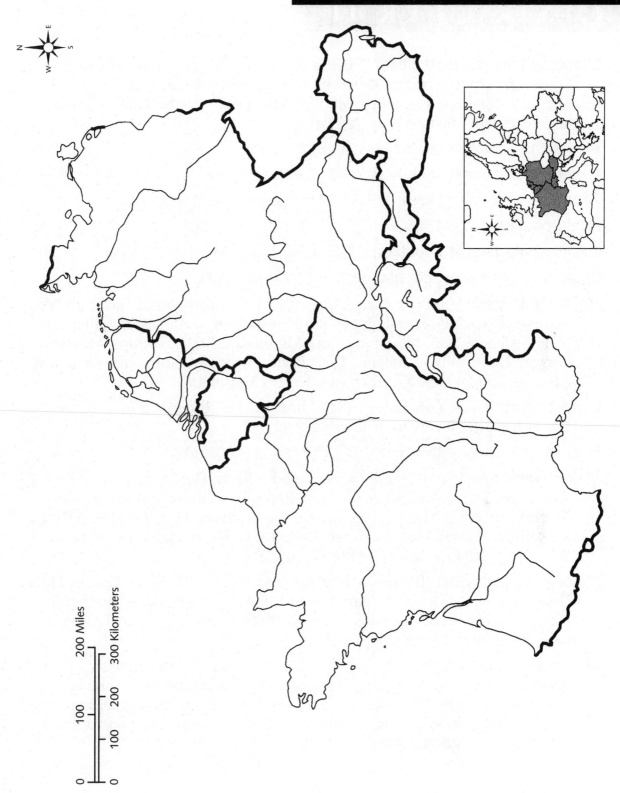

200 Miles

300 Kilometers

100   100

200

0   0

Harcourt Brace School Publishers

FACTS ABOUT
CENTRAL EUROPE

Countries (and ✪capital cities): Austria (✪Vienna), Belgium (✪Brussels), France (✪Paris), Germany (✪Berlin), Liechtenstein (✪Vaduz), Luxembourg (✪Luxembourg), Monaco (✪Monaco), Netherlands (✪Amsterdam), Switzerland (✪Bern)

Total area: 424,964 square miles (1,100,657 sq km)

Country with largest area: France, 210,026 square miles (543,967 sq km)

Country with smallest area: Monaco, 0.75 square mile (1.94 sq km)

Total population: 184,184,300

Country with largest population: Germany, 84,069,000

Country with smallest population: Liechtenstein, 32,000

Major land areas: Aquitaine Basin, Ardennes, Armorican Massif, Bavarian Alps, Bernese Alps, Black Forest, Bohemian Forest, Eastern Alps, Elbe Valley, Flanders Plain, Harz Mountains, Jura Mountains, Maritime Alps, Massif Central, Odenwald Mountains, Paris Basin, Pyrenees Mountains, Rhaetian Alps, Saxon Uplands, Vienna Basin, Vosges Mountains

Lowest point: An area of reclaimed land northeast of Rotterdam in the Netherlands, 22 feet (7 m) below sea level

Highest point: Mont Blanc in France, 15,771 feet (4,807 m)

Major rivers: Aare River, Danube River, Dender River, Dordogne River, Elbe River, Ems River, Enns River, Garonne River, IJssel River, Inn River, Loire River, Main River, Marne River, Meuse (Maas) River, Moselle (Mosel) River, Mur River, Oder River, Oise River, Rhine River, Rhône River, Saône River, Schelde River, Seine River, Vechte River, Weser River

Major bodies of water: Baltic Sea, Bay of Biscay, English Channel, Gulf of Lions, IJsselmeer, Lake Constance, Lake Geneva, Lake Lucerne, Lake Neuchâtel, Mediterranean Sea, Neusiedler Lake, North Sea, North Sea Canal, Oder Lagoon, Strait of Dover, Wadden Zee

Resources, industries, and products: Grains, potatoes, fruits, vegetables, flowers, beer, wine, textiles, machinery, chemicals, oil refining, perfume, precision instruments, ceramics, plastics, watches and clocks, iron and steel, iron ore, coal, automobiles, diamond cutting, wheat, ships, furniture, corn, tourism, metals, natural gas, banking

Harcourt Brace School Publishers

THE MAP BOOK

Name _____

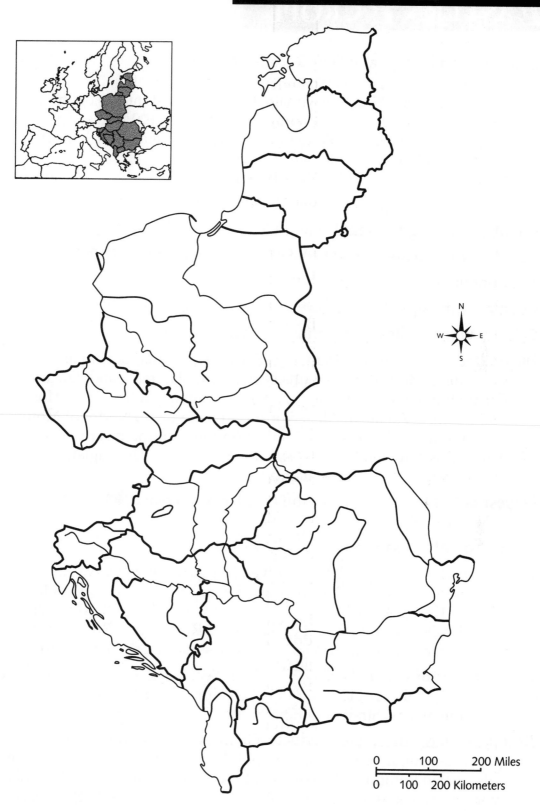

0   100   200 Miles

0   100   200 Kilometers

Harcourt Brace School Publishers

FACTS ABOUT
*E*ASTERN *E*UROPE

Countries (and ⚫capital cities): Albania (⚫Tiranë),
Bosnia and Herzegovina (⚫Sarajevo), Bulgaria (⚫Sofia),
Czech Republic (⚫Prague), Croatia (⚫Zagreb), Estonia (⚫Tallinn),
Hungary (⚫Budapest), Latvia (⚫Riga), Lithuania (⚫Vilnius),
Macedonia (⚫Skopje), Poland (⚫Warsaw), Romania (⚫Bucharest),
Slovakia (⚫Bratislava), Slovenia (⚫Ljubljana),
Yugoslavia: Serbia and Montenegro (⚫Belgrade)

Total area: 506,876 square miles (1,312,808 sq km)

Country with largest area: Poland, 120,727 square miles (312,683 sq km)

Country with smallest area: Slovenia, 7,821 square miles (20,255 sq km)

Total population: 129,561,000

Country with largest population: Poland, 38,700,000

Country with smallest population: Estonia, 1,445,000

Major land areas: Balkan Mountains, Balkan Peninsula, Bohemian Forest,
Carpathian Mountains, Danube Delta, Danubian tableland, Dinaric Alps,
Great Hungarian Plain (Alfold), Harz Mountains, Julian Alps, Moravian
Plains, North Albanian Alps, North European Plain, Northern Mountains,
Ore Mountains, Pindus Mountains, Rhodope Mountains, Riesengebirge
Mountains, Sudeten Mountains, Tatra Mountains, Thuringian Forest,
Transylvanian Alps, Transylvanian Basin

Lowest point: Inland from the Gulf of Gdańsk in Poland, 33 feet (10 m)
below sea level

Highest point: Musala in Bulgaria, 9,596 feet (2,925 m)

Major rivers: Bosna River, Danube River, Daugava River, Drava River, Drin River,
Drina River, Elbe (Labe) River, Iskur River, Kupa River, Maritsa River,
Morava River, Mures River, Neisse River, Oder River, Olt River, Prut River,
Saale River, Sava River, Siret River, Somes River, Spree River, Struma River,
Tisza River, Vardar River, Vijose River, Vistula River, Vltava River

Major bodies of water: Adriatic Sea, Baltic Sea, Black Sea, Gdańsk Bay, Gulf of
Riga, Lake Balaton, Lake Ohrid, Lake Peipus, Lake Prespa, Lake Scutari,
Pomeranian Bay, Strait of Otranto

Resources, industries, and products: Grains, potatoes, cotton, corn, sugar beets,
paper, cement, iron and steel, shipbuilding, textiles, chemicals, pharmaceuticals, coal, oil products, bauxite, food processing, wheat, carpets, timber,
machinery, metals, olives, vegetables, railway cars, oats, barley, tobacco, glass,
mercury, wood products

GREECE AND CYPRUS

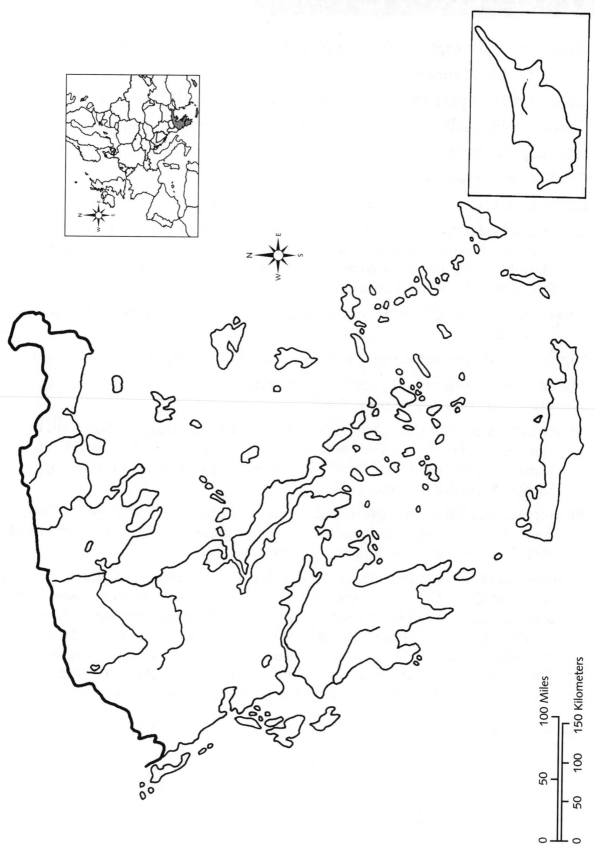

100 Miles

150 Kilometers

50

100

50

50

100

0

0

FACTS ABOUT
*G*REECE AND *C*YPRUS

Countries (and ⊙capital cities): Cyprus (⊙Nicosia), Greece (⊙Athens)

Total area: 54,521 square miles (141,208 sq km)

Country with largest area: Greece, 50,949 square miles (131,957 sq km)

Country with smallest area: Cyprus 3,572 square miles (9,251 sq km)

Total population: 11,336,000

Country with largest population: Greece, 10,583,000

Country with smallest population: Cyprus, 753,000

Major land areas: Aegean Islands, Central Plains, Ionian Islands, Larissa Plains, Olympus Mountains, Peloponnesian Lowlands, Pentadaktylos Range, Pindus Mountains, Plains of Macedonia, Plains of Thessaly, Plains of Thrace, Salonika Plain, White Plateaus

Lowest point: Along the coast of the Aegean, Ionian, and Mediterranean seas, sea level

Highest point: Mount Olympus in Greece, 9,570 feet (2,917 m)

Major rivers: Alpheus River, Mesta River, Pedias River, Pinios River, Struma River, Vardar River, Vistritsa River

Major bodies of water: Aegean Sea, Ambracian Gulf, Famagusta Bay, Gulf of Corinth, Gulf of Patras, Gulf of Salonika, Ionian Sea, Lake Kastoria, Lake Koronia, Lake Trikhonis, Larnaca Bay, Mediterranean Sea, Mirtoon Sea, Saronic Gulf, Sea of Crete

Resources, industries, and products: Citrus fruits, raisins, figs, grapes, olives, corn, potatoes, wine, food processing, sheep, goats, cotton, textiles, chemicals, metals, copper, bauxite, tourism, grains, carobs, tobacco

Unusual facts: Of the more than 2,000 Greek Isles, only 169 are inhabited. Among them are Crete, Corfu, Rhodes, Mykonos, Delos, Lesbos, Samos, Chios, Milos, and Euboea. Most of Greece's rivers dry up in the summer, because three-fourths of the total rainfall occurs in winter. In Greece there is no place that is more than 85 miles (137 km) from the sea. European civilization began in Greece more than 2,000 years ago. Many ruins from ancient times may still be seen in Greece. Among these are the Acropolis and the Parthenon.

Harcourt Brace School Publishers

THE MAP BOOK

Name _____

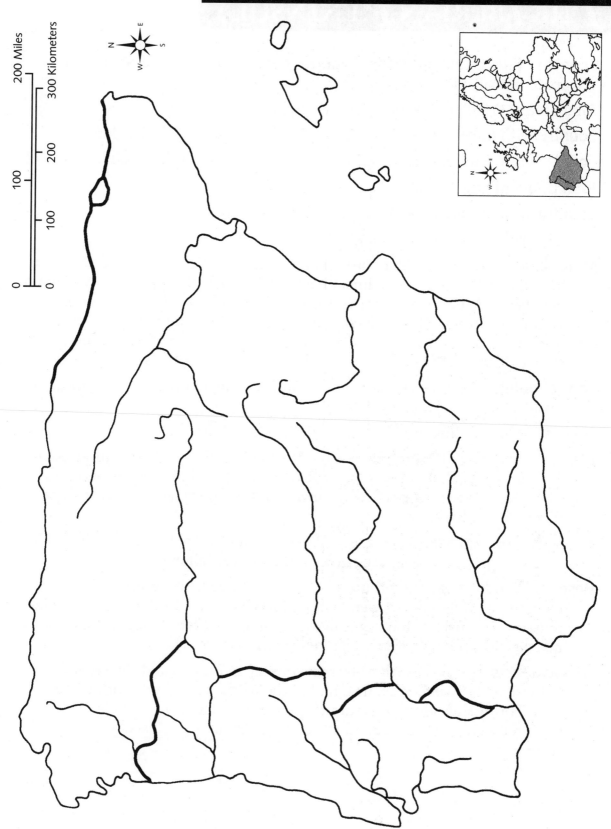

200 Miles

300 Kilometers

Harcourt Brace School Publishers

Name _____

Countries (and ✪capital cities): Andorra (✪Andorra), Portugal (✪Lisbon), Spain (✪Madrid)

Total area: 230,751 square miles (597,599 sq km)

Country with largest area: Spain, 194,897 square miles (504,782 sq km)

Country with smallest area: Andorra, 180 square miles (467 sq km)

Total population: 49,187,000

Country with largest population: Spain, 39,244,000

Country with smallest population: Andorra, 75,000

Major land areas: Andalusian Basin, Balearic Islands, Beira Litoral, Cantabrian Mountains, Catalan Mountains, Coastal plain, Ebro Basin, Iberian Mountains, Marshes of Aveiro, Mediterranean coastal belt, Meseta, Meseta Central, Montes de Toledo, Northern coastal belt, Penibética Mountains, Plains of Alentejo, Pyrenees Mountains, Serra de Estrella, Serra do Monchique, Sierra de Guadarrama, Sierra Morena, Sierra Nevada, Sintra Hills

Lowest point: Along the coasts of the Atlantic Ocean and the Mediterranean Sea, sea level

Highest point: Mulhacén in Spain, 11,407 feet (3,477 m)

Major rivers: Duero (Douro) River, Ebro River, Genil River, Guadalquivir River, Guadiana River, Jalón River, Júcar River, Miño (Minho) River, Mondego River, Sado River, Segura River, Sorraia River, Tagus (Tejo) River, Tamega River, Zezere River

Major bodies of water: Balearic Sea, Bay of Biscay, Bay of Setúbal, Gulf of Cádiz, Gulf of Valencia, Mediterranean Sea, Strait of Gibraltar

Resources, industries, and products: Potatoes, citrus fruits, grapes, olives, tobacco products, cork, paper, textiles, footwear, iron, lead, chemicals, wine, tourism, rice, fish canning, automobiles, processed foods, vegetables, grains, machinery, lignite, uranium, commerce, services

Unusual facts: Spain is the third-largest country in Europe and the second-highest, after Switzerland. One half of the world's supply of cork comes from Portugal. Andorra is semi-independent under France and Spain. Children may choose to attend either a French or Spanish school.

Harcourt Brace School Publishers

Name _____

N
W   E
S

0   100   200 Miles
0   100   200   300 Kilometers

Harcourt Brace School Publishers

Name _____

FACTS ABOUT
THE ITALIAN PENINSULA/MALTA

Countries (and ✪capital cities): Italy (✪Rome), Malta (✪Valletta), San Marino (✪San Marino), Vatican City (✪Vatican City)

Total area: 116,470 square miles (301,657 sq km)

Country with largest area: Italy, 116,324 square miles (301,279 sq km)

Country with smallest area: Vatican City, 0.17 square miles (0.44 sq km)

Total population: 57,939,000

Country with largest population: Italy, 57,534,000

Country with smallest population: Vatican City, 771

Major land areas: Apennines, Campagna, Cottian Alps, Dolomites, Graian Alps, Ligurian Alps, Madonie Mountains, Maritime Alps, Mount Titano, Pennines, Plain of Catania, Plain of Foggia, Plain of Lombardy, Po River Valley, the Tirol (Tyrol), Sardinia, Sicily

Lowest point: Along the Mediterranean coast, sea level

Highest points: On the Italian side of Mont Blanc, 15,521 feet (4,731 m); Monte Rosa in Italy, 15,203 feet (4,634 m)

Major rivers: Adige River, Arno River, Piave River, Po River, Tiber River, Ticino River, Tirso River

Major bodies of water: Adriatic Sea, Comino Channels, Gulf of Genoa, Gulf of Naples, Gulf of Salerno, Gulf of Taranto, Gulf of Venice, Ionian Sea, Lake Bolsena, Lake Como, Lake Garda, Lake Maggiore, Lake Trasimene, Ligurian Sea, Malta Channel, Mediterranean Sea, Porto Torres, St. Paul's Bay, Strait of Bonifacio, Strait of Messina, Strait of Otranto, Strait of Sicily, Tyrrhenian Sea, Valletta Harbors

Resources, industries, and products: Wheat, potatoes, olives, grapes, citrus fruits, tomatoes, woolen goods, ceramics, machinery, automobiles, steel, chemicals, textiles, shoes, cement, mercury, potash, tourism, postage stamps, food and beverages, vegetables, sulphur, cattle, pigs, sheep

Unusual facts: Mt. Etna, an active volcano, is located on Sicily. Sicily is the largest island in the Mediterranean Sea. Vatican City is the smallest independent state in the world. The city of Venice has canals instead of streets; its people use boats in place of cars and buses.

Harcourt Brace School Publishers

Name _____

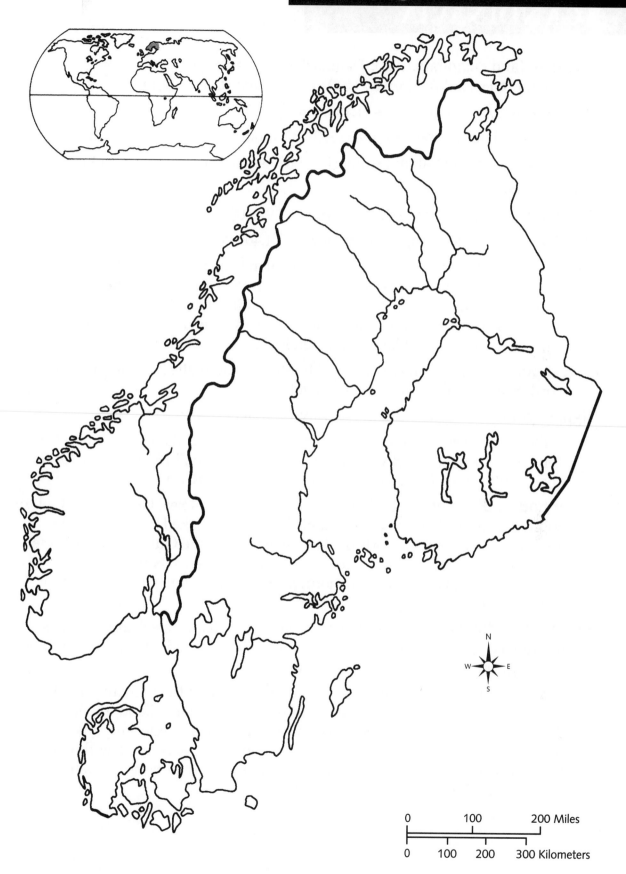

N
W   E
S

0		100		200 Miles

0   100   200   300 Kilometers

FACTS ABOUT

SCANDINAVIA

Countries (and ✪capital cities): Denmark (✪Copenhagen), Finland (✪Helsinki), Norway (✪Oslo), Sweden (✪Stockholm)

Total area: 445,980 square miles (1,155,088 sq km)

Country with largest area: Sweden, 173,732 square miles (449,966 sq km)

Country with smallest area: Denmark, 16,639 square miles (43,095 sq km)

Total population: 23,729,000

Country with largest population: Sweden, 8,946,000

Country with smallest population: Norway, 4,405,000

Major land areas: Baltic Shield, Central Swedish Depression, Coastal plains, Dovrefjell, Finnmark Plateau, Jostedalsbreen Plateau, Jotunheimen Mountains, Jutland Peninsula, Kjolen Mountains, Lake Plateau, Lapland lowland, Rondane massif, Salpaus Ridge, Skane lowlands, Smaland upland, Southern Swedish Highlands, Suomen Ridge, Uppsala Plain

Lowest point: Along the coasts of the Atlantic Ocean, Baltic Sea, Gulf of Bothnia, North Sea, and the Skagerrak, sea level

Highest point: The Glittertind in Norway, 8,110 feet (2,472 m)

Major rivers: Angerman River, Dal River, Glama River, Gota River, Guden River, Kemi River, Kokemaki River, Lagen River, Lule River, Muonio River, Orkla River, Oulu River, Ounas River, Tornio River, Ume River

Major bodies of water: Arctic Ocean, Baltic Sea, Barents Sea, Gota Canal, Gulf of Bothnia, Gulf of Finland, Imatra Rapids, Kattegat, Lake Hjalmaren, Lake Inari, Lake Malaren, Lake Mjosa, Lake Näsijärvi, Lake Oulu, Lake Paijanne, Lake Pielinen, Lake Saimaa, Lake Vanern, Lake Vattern, North Sea, Norwegian Sea, Oresund, Oslo Fjord, Skagerrak, Sogne Fjord, Trondheim Fjord, Vest Fjord

Resources, industries, and products: Shipbuilding, paper, steel, automobiles, machinery, textiles, furniture, electronics, oil, dairy products, grains, potatoes, clothing, zinc, iron, salt, metals, copper

Unusual facts: In Denmark there is no place that is more than 45 miles (72 km) from the shore. Denmark has 406 islands, including Greenland, the largest in the world. One third of Norway lies above the Arctic Circle, and it is the northernmost land in Europe. Parts of Sweden and Norway lie within a region called the Land of the Midnight Sun. In this region the sun shines 24 hours a day during parts of the summer.

Harcourt Brace School Publishers

Name _____

THE COMMONWEALTH OF INDEPENDENT STATES

1,000 Miles

500

1,000 Kilometers

500

0

0

Harcourt Brace School Publishers

FACTS ABOUT
THE COMMONWEALTH OF INDEPENDENT STATES

Countries (and ✪capital cities): Armenia (✪Yerevan), Azerbaijan (✪Baku), Belarus (✪Minsk), Georgia (✪Tbilisi), Kazakhstan (✪Almaty), Kyrgyzstan (✪Bishkek), Moldova (✪Chisinau), Russia (✪Moscow), Tajikistan (✪Dushanbe), Turkmenistan (✪Askgabat), Ukraine (✪Kiev), Uzbekistan (✪ Tashkent)

Total area: 8,533,105 square miles (22,099,035 sq km)

Country with largest area: Russia, 6,592,800 square miles (17,075,352 sq km)

Country with smallest area: Armenia, 11,500 square miles (29,783 sq km)

Total population: 285,501,000

Country with largest population: Russia, 147,987,000

Country with smallest population: Armenia, 3,466,000

Major land areas: Altai Mountains, Baltic Plain, Carpathian Mountains, Caucasus Mountains, Central Siberian Plateau, Cherski Range, Crimean Peninsula, Kamchatka Peninsula, Kara-Kum Desert, Kirgiz Steppe, Kola Peninsula, Kolyma Range, Northern European Plain, The Pamirs, Sayan Mountains, Taimyr Peninsula, Ural Mountains, West Siberian Plain, Verkhoyansk Range, Yablonovyy Range

Lowest point: Karagy Depression, 433 feet (132 m) below sea level

Highest point: Communism Peak, 24,590 feet (7,495 m)

Major rivers: Aldan River, Amu Darya River, Amur River, Dnieper River, Dniester River, Don River, Irtysh River, Lena River, Northern Dvina River, Ob River, Oka River, Syr Darya River, Volga River, Western Dvina River, Yenisey River

Major bodies of water: Aral Sea, Arctic Ocean, Barents Sea, Bering Sea, Bering Strait, Black Sea, Caspian Sea, Chukchi Sea, East Siberian Sea, Gulf of Finland, Gulf of Ob, Gulf of Sakhalin, Kara Sea, Kuril Strait, Lake Baikal, Lake Balkhash, Lake Ladoga, Lake Onega, Laptev Sea, Sea of Azov, Sea of Okhotsk, Tatar Strait, White Sea

Resources, industries, and products: Wheat, barley, sugar beets, potatoes, cotton, machinery, steel, chemicals, tractors, textiles, cement, coal, oil, iron, manganese, salt, gold, tobacco, wine, mining, figs, copper, grain, cattle, food processing, citrus fruits, grapes, motor vehicles, lead, sulfur, rice, silk, tourism

Unusual facts: Lake Baikal is the world's deepest lake, 5,715 feet (1,742 m). The Caspian Sea is 746 miles (1,200 km) long and 270 miles (434 km) wide. This makes it the largest inland body of water in the world.

Harcourt Brace School Publishers

THE MAP BOOK

Name _____

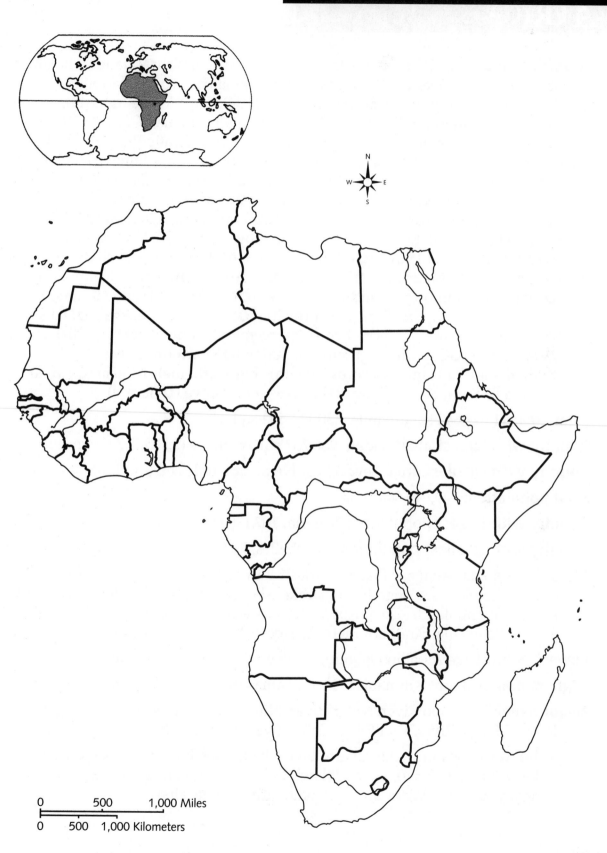

N
W E
S

Harcourt Brace School Publishers

0   500   1,000 Miles
0   500   1,000 Kilometers

FACTS ABOUT
*A*FRICA

Countries (and ✪capital cities): Algeria (✪Algiers), Angola (✪Luanda), Benin (✪Porto-Novo), Botswana (✪Gaborone), Burkina Faso (✪Ouagadougou), Burundi (✪Bujumbura), Cameroon (✪Yaoundé), Cape Verde (✪Praia), Central African Republic (✪Bangui), Chad (✪N'Djamena), Comoro Islands (✪Moroni), Republic of Congo (✪Brazzaville), Democratic Republic of the Congo (✪Kinshasa), Djibouti (✪Djibouti), Egypt (✪Cairo), Equatorial Guinea (✪Malabo), Eritrea (✪Asmara), Ethiopia (✪Addis Ababa), Gabon (✪Libreville), Gambia (✪Banjul), Ghana (✪Accra), Guinea (✪Conakry), Guinea-Bissau (✪Bissau), Ivory Coast [Côte d'Ivoire] (✪Yamoussoukro), Kenya (✪Nairobi), Lesotho (✪Maseru), Liberia (✪Monrovia), Libya (✪Tripoli), Madagascar (✪Antananarivo), Malawi (✪Lilongwe), Mali (✪Bamako), Mauritania (✪Nouakchott), Mauritius (✪Port Louis), Morocco (✪Rabat), Mozambique (✪Maputo), Namibia (✪Windhoek), Niger (✪Niamey), Nigeria (✪Abuja), Rwanda (✪Kigali), São Tomé and Príncipe (✪São Tomé), Senegal (✪Dakar), Seychelles (✪Victoria), Sierra Leone (✪Freetown), Somalia (✪Mogadishu), South Africa (✪Cape Town, Pretoria), Sudan (✪Khartoum), Swaziland (✪Mbabane), Tanzania (✪Dar es Salaam), Togo (✪Lomé), Tunisia (✪Tunis), Uganda (✪Kampala), Zambia (✪Lusaka), Zimbabwe (✪Harare)

Total area: 11,627,642 square miles (30,115,592 sq km)

Country with largest area: Sudan, 966,757 square miles (2,503,707 sq km)

Country with smallest area: Seychelles, 176 square miles (456 sq km)

Total population: 749,049,000

Country with largest population: Nigeria, 107,130,000

Country with smallest population: Seychelles, 78,000

Major land areas: Ahaggar Plateau, Atlas Mountains, Cape of Good Hope, Coastal Lowlands, Congo Basin, Drakensberg Mountains, Eastern Highlands, Ethiopian Highlands, Great Rift Valley, Ruwenzori Range, Saharan Plateau, Somali Peninsula, Southern Plateau, Tibesti Massif, Western Plateau

Lowest point: Lake Assal in Djibouti, 512 feet (156 m) below sea level

Highest point: Mount Kilimanjaro in Tanzania, 19,340 feet (5,895 m)

Major rivers: Limpopo River, Niger River, Nile River, Orange River, Senegal River, Ubangi River, Vaal River, Zaire River, Zambezi River

Major bodies of water: Lake Albert, Lake Chad, Lake Edward, Lake Kariba, Lake Nasser (artificial), Lake Malawi, Lake Rudolf, Lake Tana, Lake Tanganyika, Lake Victoria, Lake Volta, Strait of Gibraltar

Harcourt Brace School Publishers

THE MAP BOOK

Name _____

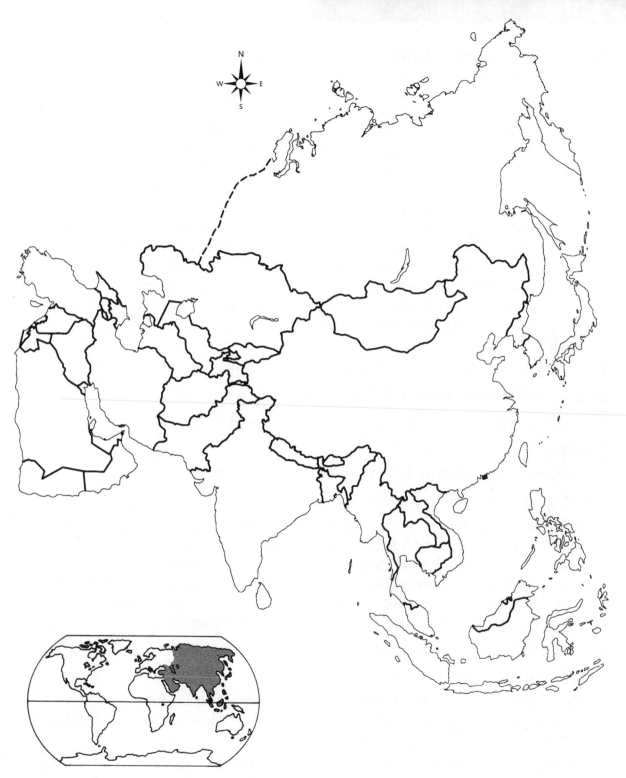

N
W — E
S

Harcourt Brace School Publishers

| 0 | 500 | 1,000 Miles |

| 0 | 500 1,000 Kilometers |

FACTS ABOUT
ASIA

Countries (and ✪capital cities): Afghanistan (✪Kabul), Armenia (✪Yerevan), Azerbaijan (✪Baku), Bahrain (✪Manama), Bangladesh (✪Dhaka), Bhutan (✪Thimphu), Brunei (✪Bandar Seri Begawan), Burma [Myanmar] (✪Rangoon [Yangôn]), Cambodia (✪Phnom Penh), China (✪Beijing), Cyprus (✪Nicosia), Georgia (✪Tbilisi), India (✪New Delhi), Indonesia (✪Jakarta), Iran (✪Tehran), Iraq (✪Baghdad), Israel (✪Jerusalem), Japan (✪Tokyo), Jordan (✪Amman), Kazakhstan (✪Aqmola), Kuwait (✪Kuwait City), Kyrgyzstan (✪Bishkek), Laos (✪Vientiane), Lebanon (✪Beirut), Malaysia (✪Kuala Lumpur), Maldives (✪Male), Mongolia (✪Ulaanbaatar), Nepal (✪Kathmandu), North Korea (✪P'yongyang), Oman (✪Muscat), Pakistan (✪Islamabad), Philippines (✪Manila), Qatar (✪Doha), Russia (✪Moscow), Saudi Arabia (✪Riyadh), Singapore (✪Singapore), South Korea (✪Seoul), Sri Lanka (✪Colombo), Syria (✪Damascus), Taiwan (✪Taipei), Tajikistan (✪Dushanbe), Thailand (✪Bangkok), Turkey (✪Ankara), Turkmenistan (✪Askgabat), United Arab Emirates (✪Abu Dhabi), Uzbekistan (✪Tashkent), Vietnam (✪Hanoi), Yemen (✪Sanaa)

Total area: 17,215,329 square miles (44,584,259 sq km)

Country with largest area: Asian Russia, 4,895,000 square miles (12,678,000 sq km)

Country with smallest area: Maldives, 115 square miles (298 sq km)

Total population: 3,640,850,000

Country with largest population: China, 1,221,592,000

Country with smallest population: Maldives, 280,000

Major land areas: Altai Mts., Anatolian Plateau, Arabian Peninsula, Caucasus Mts., Central Siberian Upland, Chang Jiang Lowland, Elburz Mts., Himalaya Mts., Hindu Kush, Indian Peninsula, Indochina Peninsula, Indo-Gangetic Plain, Karakoram, Kirgiz Steppe, Kunlun Shan, North China Plain, Pamir Mts., Plateau of Iran, Plateau of Mongolia, Plateau of Tibet, Qin Ling Mts., Taurus Mts., Tian Shan, Ural Mts., West Siberian Plain

Lowest point: The Dead Sea, 1,312 feet (400 m) below sea level

Highest point: Mount Everest, 29,028 feet (8,848 m)

Major rivers: Amur R., Brahmaputra R., Chang Jiang, Chao Phraya, Euphrates R., Ganges R., Huang He, Indus R., Irrawaddy R., Jordan R., Lena R., Mekong R., Ob R., Salween R., Tigris R., Xi Chiang, Yenisey R.

Major bodies of water: Aral Sea, Bay of Bengal, Caspian Sea, Dead Sea, Gulf of Aden, Gulf of Oman, Gulf of Tonkin, Koko Nor, Lake Baikal, Lake Balkhash, Lake Van, Persian Gulf, Sea of Galilee

Harcourt Brace School Publishers

CENTRAL ASIA

0 100 200 300 400 Miles

0 200 400 600 Kilometers

N E W S

Name _____

FACTS ABOUT
CENTRAL ASIA

Countries (and ✪capital cities): China (✪Beijing), Mongolia (✪Ulaanbaatar), Taiwan (✪Taipei)

Total area: 4,314,869 square miles (11,175,510 sq km)

Country with largest area: China, 3,696,100 square miles (9,572,899 sq km)

Country with smallest area: Taiwan, 13,969 square miles (36,177 sq km)

Total population: 1,245,786,000

Country with largest population: China, 1,221,592,000

Country with smallest population: Mongolia, 2,538,000

Major land areas: Altai Mountains, Chang Jiang Lowland, Chang Tang, Da Hinggan Ling, Gobi (Desert), Guangzhou Plain, Himalaya Mountains, Karakoram Mountains, Kunlun Shan, Leizhou Bandao, Liaodong Bandao, Manchurian Plain, Mongolian Plateau, Nan Shan Range, North China Plain, Qin Ling Mountains, Qing Zang, Shandong Bandao, Shansi Plateau, Sichuan Basin, Taipei Basin, Takla Makan (Desert), Tarim Basin, Tian Shan Range, Yunnan Kweichow Plateau

Lowest point: Turfan Depression in China, 426 feet (130 m) below sea level

Highest point: Mount Everest on the Tibet-Nepal border in China, 29,028 feet (8,848 m)

Major rivers: Amur River, Brahmaputra River, Chang Jiang, Han River, Hsiang River, Huang He (Yellow River), Kerulen River, Liao River, Mekong River, Min River, Orhon River, Salween (Nu) River, Selenga River, Songhua Jiang, Tarim He, Wei He, Xi Jiang, Yuan Jiang

Major bodies of water: Amoy Bay, Bashi Channel, East China Sea, Formosa (Taiwan) Strait, Grand Canal, Gulf of Chihli (Po Hai), Gulf of Tonkin, Hainan Strait, Hovsgol Nur, Lop Nur Lake, Namu Lake, Poyang Hu, Qingha Hu, Songhua Jiang Reservoir, South China Sea, Tungting Lake, Uvs Nur, Yellow Sea

Resources, industries, and products: Rice, cotton, tea, sugarcane, fruit, vegetables, pigs, iron and steel, textiles, clothing, chemicals, electronics, coal, oil, tin, tungsten, grain, copper, bananas, marble, silk, food processing, mining, cement, cattle, sheep, limestone, fishing

THE MAP BOOK

EASTERN ASIA

N
W ✦ E
S

Harcourt Brace School Publishers

0   50   100   150 Miles

0   100   200 Kilometers

FACTS ABOUT
*E*ASTERN *A*SIA

Countries (and ⊘capital cities): Japan (⊘Tokyo), North Korea (⊘P'yongyang), South Korea (⊘Seoul)

Total area: 231,579 square miles (599,790 sq km)

Country with largest area: Japan, 145,850 square miles (377,752 sq km)

Country with smallest area: South Korea, 38,330 square miles (99,267 sq km)

Total population: 195,982,000

Country with largest population: Japan, 125,717,000

Country with smallest population: North Korea, 24,317,000

Major land areas: Akaishi Mountains, Changpai Mountains, Han River Plain, Hida (Japan Alps), Hidaka Range, Kanto Plain, Noto Peninsula, Shikoku Range, Sobaek Range

Islands of Japan: Hokkaido, Honshu, Kyushu, Shikoku

Lowest point: Along the coasts, sea level

Highest point: Mount Fuji in Japan, 12,388 feet (3,776 m)

Major rivers: Changjin River, Han River, Imjin River, Ishikari River, Kitikami River, Kum River, Naktong River, Pujon River, Shinano River, Somjin River, Taedong River, Tone River, Tumen River, Yalu River

Major bodies of water: Amakusa Sea, Bungo Strait, Changjin Reservoir, Cheju Strait, East China Sea, Enshu Bay, Inland Sea, Ise Bay, Kanghwa Bay, Korea Bay, Korea Strait, Kumano Bay, La Pérouse Strait, Lake Biwa, Osaka Bay, Osumi Strait, Pujon Reservoir, Sea of Japan, Sea of Okhotsk, Suo Sea, Tokyo Bay, Tosa Bay, Toyama Bay, Tsugaru Strait, Uchiura Bay, Wakasa Bay, Yellow Sea

Resources, industries, and products: Rice, grains, corn, soybeans, potatoes, fruits and vegetables, fishing, chemicals, machinery, electronics, textiles, clothing, coal, copper, zinc, lead, gold, automobiles, barley, cattle, pigs, food processing, salt, ships, tungsten

Unusual facts: Lake Kutoharo in Japan is the clearest lake in the world, with a transparency of 135 feet (41 m). There are more than 3,000 Korean Islands. Cheju Island, which covers about 700 square miles (1,800 sq km), is the largest Korean Island.

Harcourt Brace School Publishers

Name _____

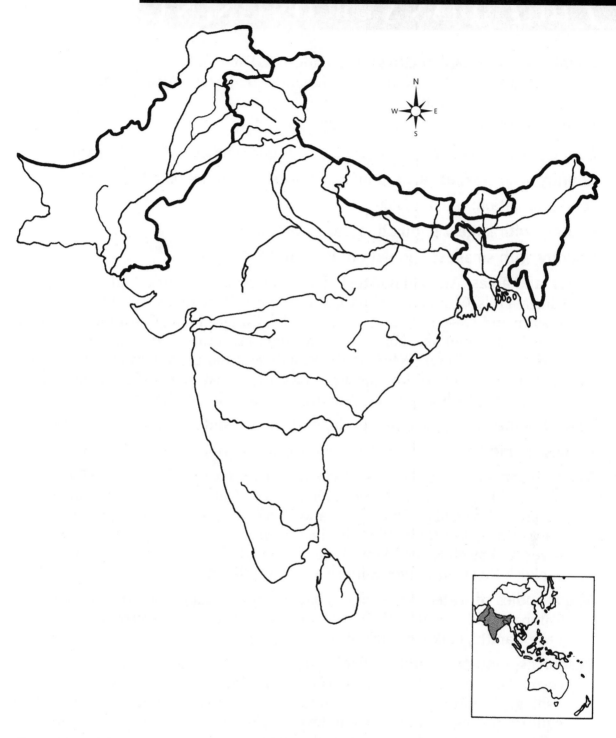

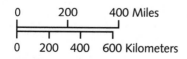

0   200   400 Miles

0   200   400   600 Kilometers

Harcourt Brace School Publishers

Name _____

Countries (and ⊙capital cities): Bangladesh (⊙Dhaka), Bhutan (⊙Thimphu), India (⊙New Delhi), Nepal (⊙Kathmandu), Pakistan (⊙Islamabad), Sri Lanka (⊙Colombo)

Total area: 1,719,857 square miles (4,454,430 sq km)

Country with largest area: India, 1,222,559 square miles (3,166,428 sq km)

Country with smallest area: Bhutan, 18,147 square miles (47,001 sq km)

Total population: 1,268,407,000

Country with largest population: India, 967,613,000

Country with smallest population: Bhutan, 1,865,000

Major land areas: Aravalli Range, Baluchistan Plateau, Central Makran Range, Chagai Hills, Chittagong Hills, Chota Nagpur Plateau, Deccan Plateau, Eastern and Western Ghats, Ganges Delta, Ganges Plain, Great Indian Desert, Himalaya Mountains, Hindu Kush Mountains, Indus Delta, Karakoram Range, Khash Desert, Khasi Hills, Mahabharat Range, Makran Coast Range, Nilgiri Hills, Rann of Kutch, Satpura Range, Siahan Range, Sulaiman Range, Thar Desert, Valley of Nepal, Vindhya Range, Wakhan Valley

Lowest point: Along the coasts of the Arabian Sea and Indian Ocean, sea level

Highest point: Mount Everest between Nepal and Tibet, 29,028 feet (8,848 m)

Major rivers: Amu Darya (Oxus) River, Brahmaputra River, Cauvery River, Chambal River, Chenab River, Gandak River, Ganges River, Ghāghara River, Godavari River, Hari River, Helmand River, Hingol (Nal) River, Indus River, Kabul River, Kali River, Karnali River, Kosi River, Krishna River, Mahanadi River, Mahaweli River, Manas River, Murghab River, Narmada River, Sankosh River, Son River, Sutlej River, Tapti River, Tista River, Yamuna River

Major bodies of water: Arabian Sea, Bay of Bengal, Cape Comorin, Gulf of Cambay, Gulf of Kutch, Gulf of Mannar, Indian Ocean, Laccadive Sea, Lake Gandhi, Palk Bay, Palk Strait

Resources, industries, and products: Rice, jute, tea, peanuts, sugarcane, coconuts, grains, potatoes, corn, cardamom, fruits, cotton, timber, livestock, fishing, chemicals, steel, metal products, fertilizers, machinery, transportation equipment, engineering, cement, textiles, clothing, food processing, paper, oil refining, soap, furniture, handicrafts, bricks, matches, shoes, rubber, stainless steel products, manganese, copper, mica, bauxite, graphite, oil and gas, coal, limestone, iron

Harcourt Brace School Publishers

Name _____

Harcourt Brace School Publishers

400 Miles

200

600 Kilometers

400

200

0

0

Name _____

Countries (and ✪capital cities): Brunei (✪Bandar Seri Begawan), Burma [Myanmar] (✪Rangoon [Yangôn]), Cambodia (✪Phnom Penh), Indonesia (✪Jakarta), Laos (✪Vientiane), Malaysia (✪Kuala Lumpur), Philippines (✪Manila), Singapore (✪Singapore), Thailand (✪Bangkok), Vietnam (✪Hanoi)

Total area: 1,735,225 square miles (4,493,886 sq km)

Country with largest area: Indonesia, 741,052 square miles (1,919,176 sq km)

Country with smallest area: Singapore, 247 square miles (640 sq km)

Total population: 507,701,000

Country with largest population: Indonesia, 209,774,000

Country with smallest population: Brunei, 308,000

Major land areas: Annam Cordillera, Arakan Yoma Mountains, Barisan Mountains, Borneo, Cagayan Valley, Celebes, Chao Phraya Lowlands, Chin Hills, Central Cordillera, Dangrek Mountains, Indochina Peninsula, Iran Mountains, Isthmus of Kra, Java, Luzon, Malay Peninsula, Mindanao, Mekong Delta, Muller Mountains, Samar, Sierra Madre, Sumatra, Upper Kapuas Mountains

Lowest point: Along the coasts, sea level

Highest point: Hkakabo Razi in Burma, 19,295 feet (5,881 m)

Major rivers: Agno River, Agusan River, Ba River, Ca River, Cagayan River, Chao Phraya River, Da River, Digul River, Hong River, Irrawaddy River, Kampar River, Kapuas River, Kinabatangan River, Mahakam River, Mamberamo River, Mekong River, Mindanao River, Mun River, Musi River, Pahang River, Pampanga River, Rajang River, Saigon River, Salween River, Sittang River

Major bodies of water: Andaman Sea, Arafura Sea, Balabac Strait, Banda Sea, Bay of Bengal, Celebes Sea, Ceram Sea, Flores Sea, Gulf of Martaban, Gulf of Thailand, Gulf of Tonkin, Indian Ocean, Java Sea, Laguna de Bay, Lake Toba, Lamon Bay, Luzon Strait, Makassar Strait, Manila Bay, Mindanao Sea, Molucca Sea, Philippine Sea, Singapore Strait, South China Sea, Strait of Malacca, Sulu Sea, Timor Sea, Tonle Sap

Resources, industries, and products: Pineapples, coconuts, sugarcane, peanuts, corn, rice, cassava, sago, sweet potatoes, pepper, bananas, spices, rubber, cork, copra, tea, coffee, livestock, cotton, fishing, wood, palm oil, textiles, clothing, tires, oil and sugar refining, electronics, oil and gas products, food products, cement, farm machinery, handicrafts, oil and gas, gravel, stone, lead, zinc, gold, silver, gemstones, tungsten, coal, tin, bauxite, chromite

AUSTRALIA, NEW ZEALAND, AND PAPUA NEW GUINEA

Harcourt Brace School Publishers

Name _____

Countries (and ✪capital cities): Australia (✪Canberra), New Zealand (✪Wellington), Papua New Guinea (✪Port Moresby)

Total area: 3,249,358 square miles (8,415,187 sq km)

Country with largest area: Australia, 2,966,200 square miles (7,681,865 sq km)

Country with smallest area: New Zealand, 104,454 square miles (270,515 sq km)

Total population: 26,522,000

Country with largest population: Australia, 18,439,000

Country with smallest population: New Zealand, 3,587,000

Major land areas: Arnhem Land, Bismarck Archipelago, Cape York Peninsula, Gibson Desert, Great Artesian Basin, Great Dividing Range, Great Sandy Desert, Great Victoria Desert, Kimberley Plateau, Macdonnell Ranges, Nullarbor Plain, Southern Alps, Swanland

Lowest point: Lake Eyre in Australia, 52 feet (16 m) below sea level

Highest point: Mount Wilhelm in Papua New Guinea, 14,762 feet (4,499 m)

Major rivers: Ashburton River, Clutha River, Darling River, Fitzroy River, Fly River, Lachlan River, Mitchell River, Murray River, Murrumbidgee River, Ramu River, Sepik River, Strickland River, Victoria River, Waikato River

Major bodies of water: Arafura Sea, Bass Strait, Bay of Plenty, Cook Strait, Coral Sea, Foveaux Strait, Great Australian Bight, Gulf of Carpentaria, Gulf of Papua, Hauraki Gulf, Hawke Bay, Indian Ocean, Lake Taupo, Lake Te Anau, Pacific Ocean, Solomon Sea, Tasman Bay, Tasman Sea, Timor Sea, Torres Strait

Resources, industries, and products: Coffee, cocoa, sugarcane, fruit, wheat, barley, oats, vegetables, sheep, cattle, wool, food processing, textiles, chemicals, machinery, iron, copper, gold, coal, oil, natural gas, uranium, fish, electrical equipment, forest products, grain, coconuts, silver, automobiles, aircraft, ships

Unusual facts: The Great Barrier Reef, off the coast of Queensland, Australia, is the world's longest coral reef (1,250 miles, or 2,000 km, long). Sutherland Falls tumbles 1,904 feet (580 m) down a mountain in New Zealand, making it one of the highest waterfalls in the world.

Harcourt Brace School Publishers

Name _____

N
W E
S

0   1,000   2,000 Miles
0   1,500   3,000 Kilometers

Harcourt Brace School Publishers

Name _____

THE WESTERN HEMISPHERE

Countries (and ✪capital cities): Antigua and Barbuda (✪St. John's), Argentina (✪Buenos Aires), Bahamas (✪Nassau), Barbados (✪Bridgetown), Belize (✪Belmopan), Bolivia (✪La Paz, Sucre), Brazil (✪Brasília), Canada (✪Ottawa), Chile (✪Santiago), Colombia (✪Bogotá), Costa Rica (✪San José), Cuba (✪Havana), Dominica (✪Roseau), Dominican Republic (✪Santo Domingo), Ecuador (✪Quito), El Salvador (✪San Salvador), Greenland—part of Denmark, Grenada (✪St. George's), Guatemala (✪Guatemala City), Guyana (✪Georgetown), Haiti (✪Port-au-Prince), Honduras (✪Tegucigalpa), Jamaica (✪Kingston), Mexico (✪Mexico City), Nicaragua (✪Managua), Panama (✪Panama City), Paraguay (✪Asunción), Peru (✪Lima), St. Kitts and Nevis (✪Basseterre), St. Lucia (✪Castries), St. Vincent and the Grenadines (✪Kingstown), Suriname (✪Paramaribo), Trinidad and Tobago (✪Port of Spain), United States (✪Washington, D.C.), Uruguay (✪Montevideo), Venezuela (✪Caracas)

Total area: 16,152,228 square miles (41,831,040 sq km)

Country with largest area: Canada, 3,849,674 square miles (9,969,886 sq km)

Country with smallest area: St. Kitts and Nevis, 104 square miles (269 sq km)

Total population: 788,009,000

Country with largest population: United States, 270,932,000

Country with smallest population: St. Kitts and Nevis, 42,000

Major land areas: *North America*—Alaska Range, Appalachian Mountains, Appalachian Plateau, Basin and Range Region, Brooks Range, Canadian Shield, Cascade Range, Central Valley (California), Coast Ranges, Colorado Plateau, Columbia Plateau, Interior Plains, Mexican Plateau, Piedmont, Rocky Mountains, Sierra Madre Occidental, Sierra Madre Oriental, Sierra Nevada, Yucatán Peninsula   *South America*—Amazon Basin, Andes Mountains, Brazilian Highlands, Cape Horn, Central Plains, Guiana Highlands, Isthmus of Panama, Pacific Coastlands, Patagonian Plateau

Lowest point: Death Valley in the U.S., 282 feet (86 m) below sea level

Highest point: Mount Aconcagua in Argentina, 22,834 feet (6,960 m)

Major rivers: Amazon River, Colorado River, Columbia River, Mackenzie River, Madeira River, Mississippi River, Missouri River, Nelson River, Ohio River, Orinoco River, Paraguay River, Paraná River, Rio Grande, Río de la Plata, St. Lawrence River, Uruguay River, Yukon River

Major bodies of water: Caribbean Sea, Great Bear Lake, Great Salt Lake, Great Slave Lake, Gulf of Mexico, Hudson Bay, Lake Athabasca, Lake Erie, Lake Huron, Lake Maracaibo, Lake Michigan, Lake Nicaragua, Lake Ontario, Lake Superior, Lake Titicaca, Lake Winnipeg

Harcourt Brace School Publishers

THE MAP BOOK

Name _____

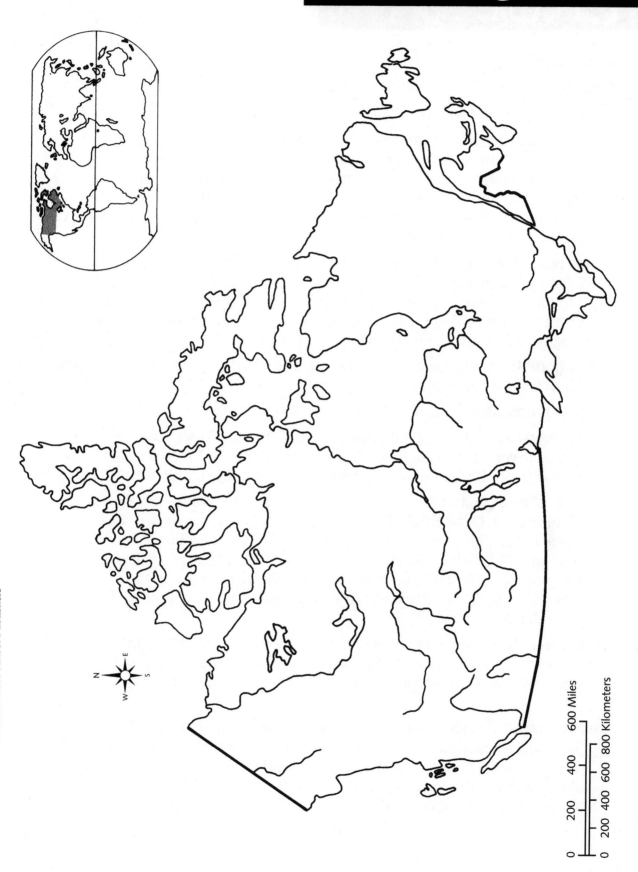

Harcourt Brace School Publishers

600 Miles

800 Kilometers

200   400

0   200   400   600

0

Name _____

FACTS ABOUT
CANADA

Population: 29,123,000

Capital: Ottawa

Total area: 3,849,674 square miles (9,969,886 sq km)

Provinces and Territories (and ✪capital cities): Alberta (✪Edmonton), British Columbia (✪Victoria), Manitoba (✪Winnipeg), New Brunswick (✪Fredericton), Newfoundland (✪St. John's), Northwest Territories (✪Yellowknife), Nova Scotia (✪Halifax), Nunavut (✪Iqaluit), Ontario (✪Toronto), Prince Edward Island (✪Charlottetown), Québec (✪Québec), Saskatchewan (✪Regina), Yukon Territory (✪Whitehorse)

Major land areas: Appalachian Highlands, Arctic Islands and Queen Elizabeth Islands (Baffin, Banks, Devon, Ellesmere, Victoria), Canadian Shield, Coast Mountains, Great Lakes–St. Lawrence Lowlands, Hudson Bay Lowlands, Interior Plains, Labrador Highlands, Newfoundland, Rocky Mountains, Ungava Peninsula, Yukon Plateau

Lowest points: Along the coasts of the Atlantic, Pacific, and Arctic oceans and Hudson Bay, sea level

Highest point: Mount Logan, 19,550 feet (6,050 m)

Major rivers: Albany River, Athabasca River, Churchill River, Columbia River, Fraser River, Mackenzie River, Nelson River, Ottawa River, Peace River, St. Lawrence River, Saskatchewan River, Severn River, Yukon River

Major bodies of water: Arctic Ocean, Athabasca Lake, Baffin Bay, Bay of Fundy, Beaufort Sea, Davis Strait, Foxe Basin, Grand Banks, Great Bear Lake, Great Slave Lake, Gulf of St. Lawrence, Hudson Bay, Hudson Strait, James Bay, Labrador Sea, Lake Erie, Lake Huron, Lake Manitoba, Lake Nipigon, Lake Ontario, Lake Superior, Lake Winnipeg, Lake Winnipegosis, Lake of the Woods, St. Lawrence Seaway, Strait of Belle Isle, Strait of Juan de Fuca, Thunder Bay, Ungava Bay

Resources, industries, and products: Transportation equipment, machinery, chemicals, paper, iron and steel, food processing, mining, livestock, fish, oil and gas, lumber, dairy products, wheat, oats, barley, corn, copper, lead, zinc, nickel

Unusual facts: Canada is the second-largest country in the world, but a third of it is almost uninhabited. The Reversing Falls of Saint John may be seen in New Brunswick near the Bay of Fundy. At low tide the water falls toward the sea. At high tide a strong current rushes in from the Bay of Fundy and pushes the water backwards over the falls.

Harcourt Brace School Publishers

THE MAP BOOK

Name _____

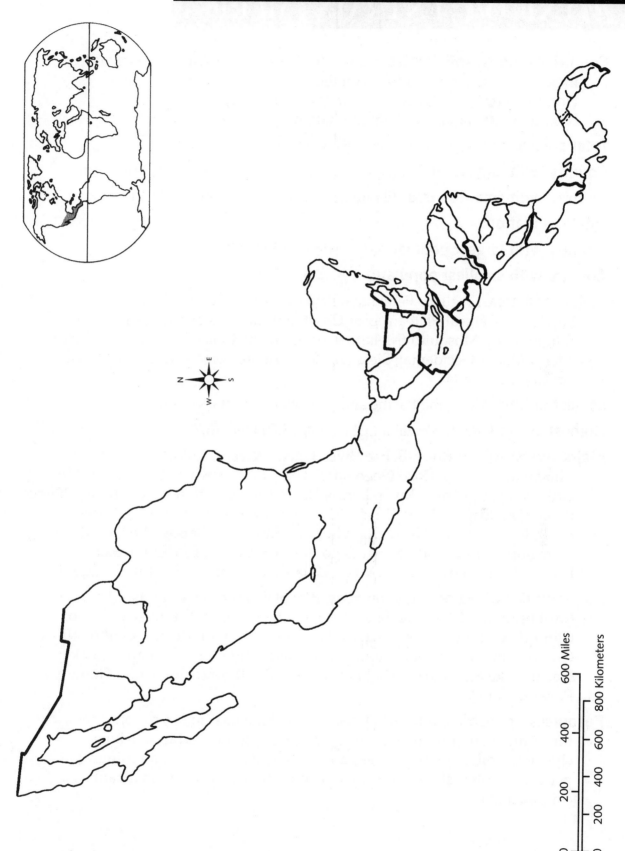

Harcourt Brace School Publishers

600 Miles

800 Kilometers

600 400 200 0

800 600 400 200 0

Name _____

Countries (and ✪capital cities): Belize (✪Belmopan), Costa Rica (✪San José), El Salvador (✪San Salvador), Guatemala (✪Guatemala City), Honduras (✪Tegucigalpa), Mexico (✪Mexico City), Nicaragua (✪Managua), Panama (✪Panama City)

Total area: 958,143 square miles (2,481,399 sq km)

Country with largest area: Mexico, 756,066 square miles (1,958,201 sq km)

Country with smallest area: El Salvador, 8,124 square miles (21,040 sq km)

Total population: 131,374,000

Country with largest population: Mexico, 97,564,000

Country with smallest population: Belize, 225,000

Major land areas: Azuero Peninsula, Baja California Peninsula, Caribbean Lowlands, Central Plateau, Gulf Coast, Isthmus of Panama, Isthmus of Tehuantepec, Mosquito (Miskito) Coast, Pacific Coastal Strip, Sierra Madre (Sierra Madre Occidental, Sierra Madre Oriental, Sierra Madre del Sur), Yucatán Peninsula

Lowest points: Along the Pacific and Caribbean coasts, sea level

Highest point: Pico de Orizaba in Mexico, 18,700 feet (5,700 m)

Major rivers: Aguán River, Belize River, Chepo River, Choluteca River, Chucunaque River, Coco (Segovia) River, Conchos River, Escondido River, Grijalva River, Lempa River, Lerma River, Motagua River, New River, Pánuco River, Papaloapan River, Pasión River, Patuca River, Paz River, Polochic River, Río Bravo del Norte (Rio Grande), Río de las Balsas, Río Grande de Matagalpa, Río Grande de Santiago, Río San Carlos, Río Sibun, San Juan River, Soto la Marina, Tuira River, Ulúa River, Usumacinta River, Yaquí River

Major bodies of water: Amatique Bay, Bay of Campeche, Caratasca Lagoon, Caribbean Sea, Chetumal Bay, Coronada Bay, Gulf of California, Gulf of Chiriquí, Gulf of Fonseca, Gulf of Honduras, Gulf of Mexico, Gulf of Nicoya, Gulf of Panama, Gulf of Tehuantepec, Lake Atitlán, Lake Chapala, Lake Izabal, Lake Managua, Lake Nicaragua, Lake Toronto, Mosquito Gulf, Panama Canal

Resources, industries, and products: Coffee, bananas, sugar, cotton, fruits, furniture, wood products, textiles, fertilizers, food products, fishing, chemicals, oil, natural gas, salt, gold, silver, lead, tourism, aluminum, petroleum, tires, steel, rubber, yucca, oil refining, international banking, copper, mahogany

Harcourt Brace School Publishers

Name _____

Harcourt Brace School Publishers

0   200   400   600 Miles

0   400   800 Kilometers

FACTS ABOUT
SOUTH AMERICA

Countries (and ✪capital cities): Argentina (✪Buenos Aires),
Bolivia (✪Sucre—legal, ✪La Paz—de facto), Brazil (✪Brasília),
Chile (✪Santiago), Colombia (✪Bogotá), Ecuador (✪Quito),
Guyana (✪Georgetown), Paraguay (✪Asunción), Peru (✪Lima),
Suriname (✪Paramaribo), Uruguay (✪Montevideo), Venezuela (✪Caracas)

Total area: 6,841,904 square miles (17,719,162 sq km)

Country with largest area: Brazil, 3,286,470 square miles (8,511,300 sq km)

Country with smallest area: Suriname, 63,251 square miles (163,807 sq km)

Total population: 329,005,000

Country with largest population: Brazil, 164,511,000

Country with smallest population: Suriname, 443,000

Major land areas: Altiplanos, Amazon Basin, Andes Mountains, Atacama Desert,
Brazilian Highlands, Cape Horn, Central Plains, Cordillera Central,
Cordillera Occidental, Cordillera Oriental, Falkland Islands, Gran Chaco,
Guiana Highlands, Isthmus of Panama, Llanos, Mato Grosso Plateau,
Montaña, Pacific Coastlands, Pampas, Patagonian Plateau, Selvas

Lowest point: Váldéz Peninsula in Argentina, 131 feet (40 m) below sea level

Highest point: Mount Aconcagua in Argentina, 22,834 feet (6,960 m)

Major rivers: Amazon River, Apurímac River, Arauca River, Beni River, Bío-bío
River, Cauca River, Coppename River, Courantyne River, Esmeraldas River,
Guaporé River, Guaviare River, Huallaga River, Madeira River, Madre de
Dios River, Magdalena River, Mamoré River, Marañón River, Maroni River,
Meta River, Orinoco River, Pará River, Paraguay River, Paraná River,
Pilcomayo River, Río Negro, Río de la Plata, São Francisco River, Tocantins
River, Ucayali River, Urubamba River, Uruguay River, Xingu River

Major bodies of water: Angel Falls, Atlantic Ocean, Caribbean Sea, Corcovado
Gulf, Gulf of Guayaquil, Gulf of San Jorge, Gulf of Venezuela, Lagoa dos
Patos, Lake Maracaibo, Lake Mar Chiquita, Lake Poopó, Lake Titicaca,
Peñas Gulf, Samborombón Bay, San Matías Gulf, Strait of Magellan

Resources, industries, and products: Coffee, bananas, sugarcane, grains, cotton,
fruits, wool, fishing, food processing, wood products, textiles, chemicals,
steel, tin, oil, bauxite, iron, emeralds, mining, potatoes, automobiles, ships,
copper, rice, diamonds, cement, corn, paper

Harcourt Brace School Publishers

THE MAP BOOK

Name _____

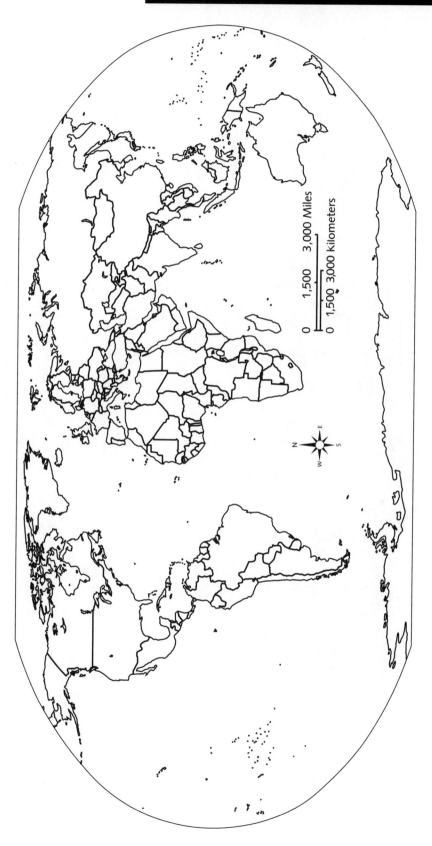

3,000 Miles

1,500

0

3,000 Kilometers

1,500

0

Harcourt Brace School Publishers

Name _____

THE WORLD—PHYSICAL

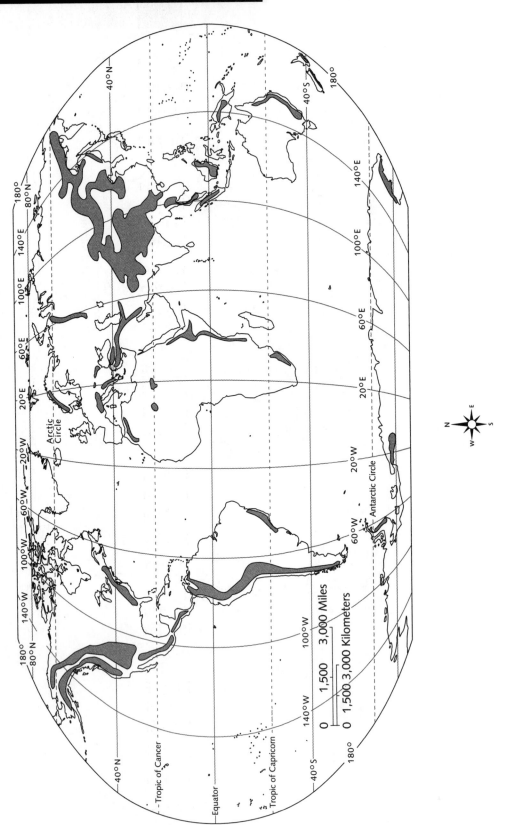

THE MAP BOOK

Harcourt Brace School Publishers

Name _____

Total area: 196,950,000 square miles (510,061,000 sq km)

Total land area: 57,800,000 square miles (149,690,000 sq km)

Total water area: 139,150,000 square miles (360,370,670 sq km)

Continents (by size): Asia, Africa, North America, South America, Antarctica, Europe, Australia

Major islands and island groups (by size): Greenland, New Guinea, Borneo, Madagascar, Baffin, Sumatra, Japan, Philippines, New Zealand, Great Britain, Victoria, Ellesmere, Celebes, Java, Newfoundland, Cuba, Luzon, Iceland, Mindanao, Moluccas Islands, Novaya Zemlya, Ireland

Major bodies of salt water (by size): Pacific Ocean, Atlantic Ocean, Indian Ocean, Arctic Ocean, South China Sea, Caribbean Sea, Mediterranean Sea, Bering Sea, Gulf of Mexico, Sea of Okhotsk, Sea of Japan, Hudson Bay, East China Sea, Andaman Sea, Black Sea, Red Sea, North Sea, Baltic Sea, Yellow Sea, Persian Gulf, Gulf of California

Ten largest lakes (by size): Caspian Sea in Asia-Europe, Lake Superior in North America, Lake Victoria in Africa, Aral Sea in Asia, Lake Huron in North America, Lake Michigan in North America, Lake Tanganyika in Africa, Lake Baykal in Asia, Great Bear Lake in North America, Lake Nyasa in Africa

Ten longest rivers (by length): Nile River in Africa, Amazon River in South America, Chang Jiang in Asia, Huang He in Asia, Ob-Irtysh River in Asia, Lena River in Asia, Congo River in Africa, Mackenzie River in North America, Mekong River in Asia, Niger in Africa

Highest waterfall: Salto Angel (Angel Falls) in South America, 3,212 feet (979 m)

Major waterfalls (by volume): Boyoma (Stanley) Falls in Africa, Sete Quedas (Guayra) in South America

Major mountain ranges: Alaska Range, Alps, Altai Mts., Andes Mts., Apennines, Appalachian Mts., Atlas Mts., Balkan Mts., Brooks Range, Carpathian Mts., Cascade Range, Caucasus Mts., Coast Ranges, Dinaric Alps, Drakensberg Mts., Himalayas, Hindu Kush, Karakoram-Kunlun-Nan Shan-Tsinling Shan Mts., Lebanon Mts., Oman Mts., Pamir Mts., Pyrenees, Rocky Mts., Ruwenzori Range, Sierra Madre Occidental, Sierra Madre Oriental, Sierra Nevada, Taurus Mts., Tien Shan, Ural Mts., Zagros Mts.

Highest mountain: Mount Everest in Asia, 29,028 feet (8,848 m)

Lowest point on land: Shore surrounding the Dead Sea in Asia, 1,312 feet (400 m) below sea level

Harcourt Brace School Publishers

FACTS ABOUT
THE WORLD

Major volcanic areas: There are more than 850 active volcanoes in the world. Most of these volcanoes are located within a zone called the Ring of Fire. The Ring of Fire includes the west coast of the Americas from Chile to Alaska and the east coast of Asia from Siberia to New Zealand. More than 20 percent of the world's active volcanoes are located in Indonesia.

Climates: The regions near the North and South poles are cold, with long winters and short summers. Yearly precipitation is less than 10 inches (25 cm). The climate is polar near the poles and subarctic near the Arctic and Antarctic circles. In the tropical lands near the equator, it is hot all year round. Yearly precipitation can be over 60 inches (152 cm). In the Tropic of Cancer and the Tropic of Capricorn, climates are subtropical, semiarid, or arid. Precipitation gets lighter as you move away from the equator. Between these Tropics and Circles, climates tend to be mild, with warm summers and cool-to-cold winters.

Major deserts: Atacama Desert, Australian Desert, Gobi, Kalahari Desert, Kara Kum, Kyzyl Kum, Libyan Desert, Negev, North American Desert, Rubʿ al Khali, Sahara, Syrian Desert, Takla Makan, Thar Desert

Major rainforest areas (by size): Amazon River Basin in South America, Congo River Basin in Africa, much of Southeast Asia

Coldest areas on an annual basis: Antarctica and Siberia

Hottest areas on an annual basis: Dallol in Ethiopia, Death Valley in California, and Marble Bay and Wyndham in Australia

Area with the highest average rainfall: Tutunendo in Colombia, 463 inches (1,176 cm) per year

Area with the lowest average rainfall: Atacama Desert in Chile, 0 inches (0 cm) per year

Major languages: Arabic, Bengali, Chinese, English, French, German, Hindi, Japanese, Malay, Portuguese, Russian, Spanish, Urdu

Major religions: Buddhism, Christianity, Hinduism, Islam, Judaism

Most abundant minerals: aluminum, chromium, cobalt, columbium, copper, gold, iron ore, lead, manganese, nickel, platinum, silver, tantalum, zinc

Major crops: barley, corn, cotton, millet, oats, rice, sorghum, wheat

Ten largest countries (by size): Russia, Canada, China, United States, Brazil, Australia, India, Argentina, Sudan, Algeria

Ten largest countries (by population): China, India, United States, Indonesia, Brazil, Russia, Japan, Nigeria, Bangladesh, Pakistan

Harcourt Brace School Publishers

Name _____

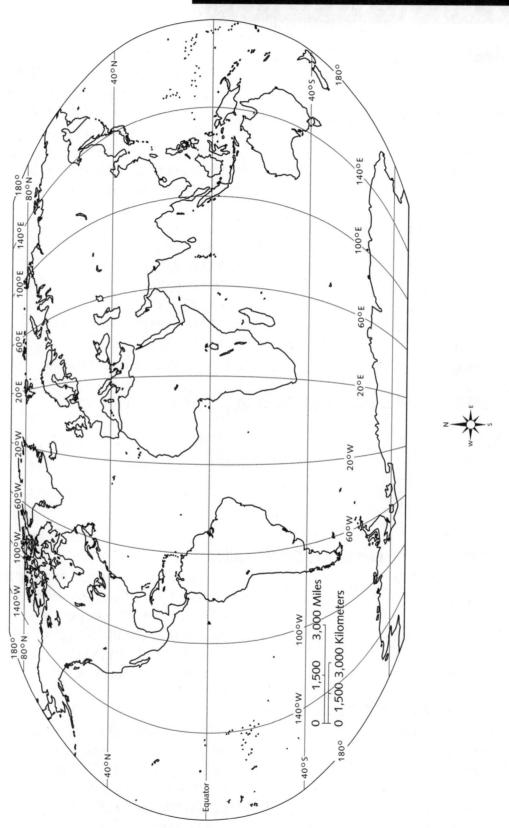

Harcourt Brace School Publishers

Name _____

THE CONTINENTS

AREA

Asia	17,012,000 square miles (44,062,000 sq km)
Africa	11,707,000 square miles (30,320,000 sq km)
North America	9,362,000 square miles (24,247,500 sq km)
South America	6,884,000 square miles (17,830,000 sq km)
Antarctica	5,500,000 square miles (14,425,000 sq km)
Europe	4,063,000 square miles (10,523,000 sq km)
Australia	2,967,700 square miles (7,686,000 sq km)

WHERE PEOPLE LIVE

Asia	3,686,850,000
Europe	792,692,000
Africa	749,049,000
North America	431,429,000
South America	329,005,000
Australia	18,439,000
Antarctica	no permanent population

POPULATION DENSITY (number of people per square mile)

Asia	206
Europe	176
Africa	61
North America	48
South America	46
Australia	6

LARGEST CITY ON EACH CONTINENT

North America	Mexico City (16 million people)
Asia	Tokyo (27 million people)
Europe	Moscow (9 million people)
South America	São Paulo (16 million people)
Africa	Cairo (9 million people)
Australia	Sydney (4 million people)

COASTLINE LENGTH

North America	190,000 miles (305,767 km)
Asia	80,205 miles (129,077 km)
Europe	37,887 miles (60,973 km)
Africa	22,921 miles (36,888 km)
South America	20,000 miles (32,000 km)
Antarctica	19,800 miles (31,900 km)
Australia	17,366 miles (27,948 km)

THE MAP BOOK

Name _____

The Western Hemisphere

The Eastern Hemisphere

Harcourt Brace School Publishers

THE MAP BOOK

Name _____

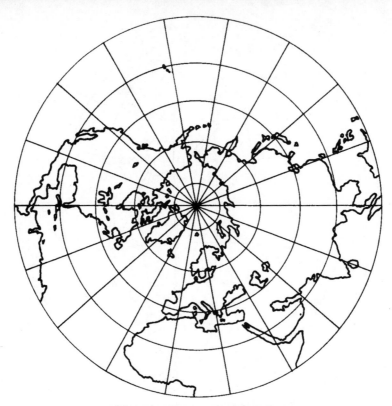

The Northern Hemisphere

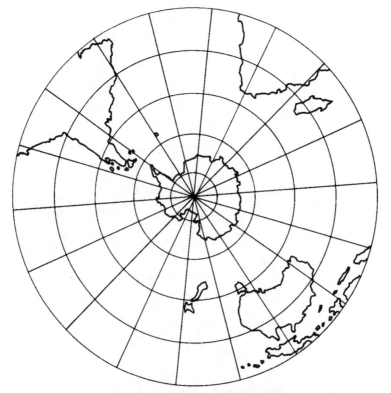

The Southern Hemisphere

Harcourt Brace School Publishers

THE MAP BOOK